Swimming in Circles

A Baby Chase Odyssey

by

Michael C. Barr

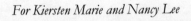

For Kiersten Marie and Nancy Lee

I get to see one every morning and I hope to see the other again one day.

PREFACE
(JANUARY 2006)

It's 1:21 in the morning and I'm sitting at our attic desktop computer. The monitor sits atop an antique sewing table because we once thought it would be a clever solution for a computer desk in this old relic of a house we own. It is horribly dysfunctional. The foot pedal that spins the gear to engage the sewing machine still works, and every time you stretch your legs you inevitably turn a ghost stitch which then rattles your monitor. Unnerving is what it is. Worse yet, it almost spilled my bourbon.

So I'm sitting here mildly inebriated and unable to sleep. The events of my day, my week, and the last several months have accumulated to a point where confusion radiates out of my eyes as if I were a stoned teenager trying to read *The Iliad*. I feel emotionally anesthetized. I see things occurring all around me that seem strange, depressing, and frequently absurd, until every aspect of my reality drains into one giant pool of untenable sludge. I can barely react anymore.

Pour a drink, put on a sweater, walk to the attic, and stare at the news on MSNBC. That's all I can think to do. I don't have anyone to talk with about this personal little hell of a situation we've gotten ourselves into. Guys don't talk about stuff like this. We talk about beer and sports and tools. We don't typically chit-chat about breeding, endometriosis, and sperm count. I can barely talk about these things with my wife. This secret, this predicament, is beginning to overwhelm me.

And this, it seems, is the confluence of circumstances that I need to process.

I'll talk to the blank page. Telling this story, putting it permanently in print, this is my cure.

This is cathartic.

You may have several moments while reading this when you wonder why anyone would write a book this self-deprecating, this embarrassing, and what I want you to know is: The story is this way simply because it's the truth. And if by telling the truth, I can help some other poor schmo who finds himself in a similar situation, and be that friend he can talk to about this unspeakable subject, then I've succeeded. If I can help a wife better understand her husband as they navigate the path of the procreation-challenged, I get a gold star. If I can make you laugh, then super. If I make you cry, then at least you're crying at someone else's expense. I apologize in advance if I offend anyone, and I suspect I might.

As I write this, I only have advance knowledge of the beginning. The middle and the end of this journey are one gaping black hole of scary for me. But what I want you to know is that having you come along with me is invigorating. Your eyes on this page give me someone to share with, and it is liberating.

This is an all-access pass into my life, and I submit it to you, naked with authenticity.

Some of the names will be changed, but the story is unwavering in its honesty, even when its truth is an uncomfortable one.

Who of us is mature enough for offspring before the offspring themselves arrive? The value of marriage is not that adults produce children but that children produce adults.

– Peter De Vries (1910-1993)

ART LESSON
(DECEMBER 2004)

Dr. Granderson drew a circle. This was no run-of-the-mill sphere. It was compass quality. Clearly, he'd done this before.

"Okay, imagine this is the egg," he said.

If he draws a penis, I'm going to giggle like a little girl.

Flanked by a reproduction antique roll-top desk that was compulsively organized with brochures and writing tablets, Granderson sat no more than a couple feet across from the puffy pink-and-white striped couch in which we were currently submerged. He slid his specs up his nose with a middle finger and clicked his mechanical pencil twice with a determination that suggested he was just getting warmed up.

"Now, these are sperm," he said.

Methodically, Granderson sketched three rugby ball objects with tails. One boasted a terrifically large head, another resembled a typical pin-head, and the last appeared to possess a perfectly proportioned oval with a flawless squiggly little accessory.

Why do I already hate that last one?

He fixated on us, eyes slightly above the frame of his glasses, and paused.

Kiersten shifted nervously on the couch.

Granderson had a kind, concerned face and a gentle demeanor, and struck me as a lifelong glass-half-full kind of guy. His expression reminded me of a man facing a challenge he'd seen before and rather enjoyed—like when my Dad used to look at the stalled engine of my 1976 Toyota Corolla, rubbing his hands together in anticipation. Lips pursed, half smiling, half frowning—kind of a pleasurable grimace.

"Imagine that the sperm are boats and they're docking... they're docking at the egg," he said.

Is my wife wearing her "I'm with stupid" shirt again?

"They need to be the perfect size to dock—to get inside," he continued. "The one with the larger head is too big; the one with the smaller head is too tiny. Only the perfectly shaped one can gain entry to the egg."

Oh, God—I've got big-headed sperm, don't I? What if they're the little-headed ones? What the hell does that mean?

The art lesson continued, Granderson's pencil furiously scribbling vertical lines and circular orbits.

"Some sperm are slow, some swim in random directions, and others don't move much at all," he posited, pencil mimicking the narrative. He lashed several lines violently across the paper, towards our imaginary dock. "Then there are sperm that are strong swimmers—these are the ones we want." The pencil tapped intently on his masterpiece for emphasis, like a woodpecker high on crack.

I've got big-headed, slow-swimming idiot sperm, don't I? Just say it. Oh, God I need water. No, I need a drink. A strong drink.

"Now, Michael—bear with me. There's good news and there's not-so-good news."

Where's the waitress? Makers Mark and rocks, please— pronto.

"Let's talk about sperm count."

More Makers, less rocks…

"You're at about 23 million sperm per millimeter…"

23 mil? It's a deep drive to right field, he goes back, a waaaay back…

"…and a normal sperm count is anywhere between 20 million and about 150 million per millimeter."

Foul ball. That can't be the good news.

"So we're doing just fine there."

Kill me.

"Your sperm movement, what we call motility, could be better. You see, sperm must be able to rapidly navigate through the cervical mucous in order to reach the egg."

Is it absolutely necessary to say mucous? Can't we just call it 'stuff'?

"Your sperm have a low rate of rapid movement and some sperm do not navigate well."

"Can you be a little more specific?" I asked. "What do you mean, they don't navigate well?"

"Well, many swim aimlessly or in circles."

I caught Kiersten glancing at me. She knew we were going to the brewery after this. She had to know.

"Now, your sperm morphology…" continued Grand-erson.

Oh, for the love of God… morpho-what?

"…could be better as well. You demonstrate a low percentage of normal sperm shape and structure."

I dare you to pick up that pencil and draw me a picture. I double dog dare you.

Kiersten started asking questions. I think they were something along the lines of 'Could we ever get pregnant on our own?' and 'Can his sperm be improved?' and 'Is my husband a pathetic, feeble little cretin and do you have any handsome virile sons you could introduce me to?' But frankly, I couldn't even hear… Their conversation had been reduced to inaudible static, as if the frequency on my radio dial was fading out of range and I had my foot flooring the gas.

The room felt like it was slowly shrinking around me.

I stood to take off my coat and realized I was not on solid ground. As if experiencing a sudden drop in blood pressure, I was hazy. Cotton mouth. Visibly sweating. A pulse so fast, I could feel the vein in my neck throb like an unwelcome kick drum under my skin. I couldn't even stomach the triple-tall-with-room Americano I had arrived with… a tragic waste of our last legal high.

I sat down and tried to look as casual as possible although I didn't know if I was about to puke, pass out, or both. Nonchalantly stroking the four o'clock stubble on my chin with my left hand, I tried to look as if I was curiously following their conversation, but in reality I was trying to stave off what could only be some kind of anxiety attack.

I tried to go to a happy place in my spiraling skull. A place where Imperial IPA is refilled by the waitress as if it were table water and double gin martinis are served complimentary with every entrée. I was brought back by a squeeze on the knee and a disapproving glare suggesting I needed to be more attentive to the current conversation.

Ok…deep breaths. Calm down… calm the hell down.

I was obsessively rubbing my damp hands on my thighs, rocking back and forth slightly, but noticeably.

Think…think…think…

This is your ticket to annual Vegas trips, to keeping up with your golf game, to turning the playroom into your own personal game room. You've never really wanted a screaming, puking, crapping, drooling, keeping-me-up-at-night, preempting-the-ballgame-for-Teletubbies-and-the-freaking-Wiggles, stealing-my-wife's-boobs, snot-nosed brat, did you?

I looked up to see Kiersten's hopeful face.

I couldn't deny that I wanted this. If not for us, at least for her. God, I love her.

"Uh…Granderson? I missed the last couple seconds…Could you go over our options again?"

As he started to reiterate the unseemly choices we faced, I couldn't help but wonder:

How the hell did I get here?

RUBBER STAMP
(FALL 1997)

I'd walked past that building dozens of times, but it was one of those places to which you never gave a second thought until you actually had a reason to go there. It was a nondescript, unassuming one-story corner building painted a hue so drab, the siding seemed to yawn. I think it used to be some kind of Indian restaurant or "Turkey House" here, back before I started college. Perhaps it was Indian turkey, who knows—but whatever they served, it clearly didn't catch on. Because today, it bore a sandpit and jungle gym for the dozens of little monsters that now called the turkey house their school—or "Day Academy," as the sign said—a name so fancy, it allowed administrators to bilk parents for thousands in annual tuition.

What brought me here was a delivery. Maggie, my boss at the time, had two small children. Apparently their teacher, who moonlighted as their occasional babysitter, had left a box of Egyptian hieroglyph stamps at her house the previous week. Maggie's kids went to this turkey-house-Day-Academy, which was conveniently situated between my house and my workplace. Convenient for Maggie, that is, because she dropped the stamps off on the porch of the house I was renting with instructions to deliver them to the babysitter-teacher-lady on Monday morning.

You're probably wondering, as I did, "*Why the hell didn't you deliver you own damn stamps when you **dropped your kids off for school?***" But I wasn't entirely sure I fit in particularly well at my workplace to begin with and as the only man in an office of twenty women, I didn't like to attract attention, so I typically did what I was told. Some of my coworkers were going through menopause, while a dozen others were cycling together, so I just tried to be as anonymous as possible. Call it an instinct for survival.

It was well before any students arrived at their "academy" and the parking lot was empty save for one little gold Toyota Paseo. I wasn't sure if anyone was even there, but the front door was open so I decided to have a look around. On the way in, it was pretty obvious where the lobby and register must have been for the restaurant, but the staff had cleverly converted this space into a mud-room of sorts where kids could hang their rainy coats and take their muddy shoes off. Water-color paintings in shapes relevant only to the artists adorned the walls. Trees, suns, and stick people seemed to be the popular themes with this generation.

"Hello?" I tentatively called out into the darkness. No response.

There was a faint light coming from one of the rooms towards the back, and I stumbled my way through a sea of beanbags, bookcases, and knee-high desks as I walked toward it. Peering in the solitary lit room, I found a young lady rearranging the desks and generally looking busy.

"Um, hello?"

"Oh! Hi," she said.

As she looked up at me, it became clear to me what Maggie was up to. The girl was a knockout.

Uh… whatever you're teaching today, I'm needing a lesson in it.

She wore a blue wool wrap-around skirt, shorter than your typical teacher's garb by a good few inches. A button-up cardigan conservatively covered her wiry but elegantly defined build. Her hair was worn on top of her head in a bun of blond curls. Her features were distinct—a square jaw bracketing a narrow face highlighted by brilliant blue eyes and a porcelain complexion—pale, but in an angelic way. I figured her for 20, maybe 21 years old.

Why couldn't MY first grade teacher have been this hot?

My usually reliable confidence betrayed me in her presence. While I was typically good for a witty comment or at least some degree of charm, all I could muster was a regurgitation of my instructions.

"Maggie asked me to return these stamps for her."

"Oh, yeah—thank you."

"She's my boss—Maggie, that is," I stammered. "She asked me to return these for her." I held them out.

"Yeah, you said that," she said, taking the stamps from me. I sheepishly shifted my eyes around the room. If I looked at her directly for longer than a few seconds, I thought my head would explode, or I would just fall in love with her.

"Thank you," she said.

"You're welcome." I smiled at her and prayed to God to give me something intelligent to say, but it seemed that the Big Guy was up to more important things than helping me relocate my suave gene. I stood in front of her briefly, grinning like an idiot and nodding my head like I'd never seen an adult woman in my life. Sensing the uncomfortable silence had lasted far too long, I waved and made a hurried exit, replaying the last sixty seconds in my head, thinking of all the things I possibly could have said to prolong the conversation.

Real freaking smooth, I thought, shaking my head and mumbling to myself all the way out the door.

It soon occurred to me that I didn't even get her name—I couldn't even deliver some kind of covert note or message for her at the school, asking her for a date. I wondered if I could somehow lurk near the playground and ask some insecure, lonely seven-year-old, *"Hey, kid—who's the hot blonde teacher? There's a Teenage Mutant Ninja Turtle lunchbox in it for you..."*

To make matters worse, I had to get back in my car, which had stopped being cool when I was about 19. It was a 1986 red Pontiac Fiero. My Dad had bought it for me in high school with savings bonds my grandparents purchased back in the early 1970s. It was between that, and a 1990 white Ford Escort which would have all but equaled instant geekdom. Why not just join the chess team? The Fiero had served me well in high school, but by now the feeling I got driving it was akin to that of those balding sixty-somethings who pony up the 40K for a Corvette with T-tops: *So fun to drive, but I must look like I'm driving it to mask my tiny penis.*

I flipped up my one working headlight and sped away, wondering if I'd ever have another opportunity to visit the school and this girl. If she saw me in this pathetic little Pontiac, I was surely sunk.

Of course, maybe I shouldn't have been trying to impress anyone to begin with. I had a girlfriend at the time, although that relationship's prospects for longevity weren't great. I came to that conclusion after our third date when she declared, "You can pretty much do anything you want to me, except put it in my ass." It's not that I was disappointed by her liberated attitude, but her statement was delivered with a nonchalance similar to the way I order my daily Americano. And I got the feeling it wasn't the first time she'd said it. Call me old fashioned, but it was tough to picture the woman raising my kids reminiscing about how she "got your father to marry me by letting him wheelbarrow me any time he wanted." This was a girl to drink beer with, not necessarily to bring home to mom.

I arrived at work, to Maggie's anticipatory, wide-eyed "what did you think of her?" looks. Deciding to sidestep what would no doubt have been a bad conversation, I went to my office to subsume myself in a sea of paperwork and various e-mails sent with high importance which really could have waited until next month. My attempt at keeping a low profile didn't last long.

"So, did you return those stamps for me?" Maggie asked, tilting her head and smiling freakishly, giddy with her own shenanigans.

"Yep, consider them delivered."

"Well…" she probed.

"Well what?"

"Well, *what did you think?!*" she said pointedly.

"I think they need better lighting in there, and it still sort of smelled like Indian food."

"Oh, Barr—come on now, you know what I'm talking about."

"You set me up!" I said indignantly.

"Well, she's available!"

"Oh, and because she's available, you think a girl with those kinds of looks is going to fall for the *stamp delivery boy*?"

"Stranger things have happened," she said.

"That gives me tremendous confidence."

Maggie threw her hands in the air, exasperated, and left my office.

Well, that should be the last time she sets me up.

The next morning, I walked into my office to discover a beaming Maggie waiting there for me.

"Let me guess, you want me to take a load of your trash to the garbage because the dump girl is hot and single?"

"I picked the kids up from school last night," she said.

"Boy, you're doing overtime on that mother-of-the-year award, aren't you?"

My sarcasm didn't even dent her armor—she was on a mission.

"And she said, 'I'm going to leave more things at your house if you're going to send cute boys to deliver them.'"

"Who did?"

"SHE did."

"She did?"

"So I asked her if I could give you her number!" she said, entirely too proudly.

"You did not."

"I did," she said, handing me a piece of paper.

I opened it up. Seven digits. *Kiersten* was her name.

ISSUES

Kiersten and I had been married just under seven years. I was 32, she was 29. Up to this point in our lives, we had primarily focused on us, careers, advanced degrees, and eating at restaurants as much as possible. Our marriage was pretty much one never-ending date interrupted by our occupations. Most days consisted of work, then drinks, dinner out, more drinks, and things that too many drinks, empty wallets, hormones, and your own house with no kids lead to. We'd drag ourselves to work and do it all over again the following day.

Kids were always a *when*, never an *if* or a *maybe*. We always knew we would have children; we were just never sure about the timing, agreeing that 'you're never really ready for a baby.' We had a plan all along—one biological, then one adopted, preferably international. We were committed to the plan, but neither of us had a strong sense of when such a plan should be executed. Any clarity this plan may have possessed tended to get lost in bottles of gin and stacks of overdraft statements from the bank. It was tough to thoughtfully plan for children when you were dirt poor and hung over.

Personal and financial issues aside, I left the decision almost entirely up to her: her body, her decision. Each year, I think the clock ticked a little louder. In fact, for some time, I thought she was about to open her own library of baby-name books.

"What do you think of the name Clementine?"

"Do you like the name Pearl?"

"I love the name Flora."

"What do you think of the name Harriet? We could call her Hattie."

Clearly, the time had come. Or at least we needed to name something.

We understood this kid thing might not be a snap. Kiersten had a long history of ovarian cysts which had left a trail of scar tissue throughout her abdomen, causing undue discomfort on an ongoing basis. The pain got so bad at one point that she even had a laparoscopy to shave down the scar tissue. But in general, the soreness could be kept in moderate check by maintaining a regimen of birth control pills. According to expert opinion, those are bad for making babies, and therein lay the big problem.

There was also a family legacy of endometriosis, which might be the fancy word for the discomfort she was experiencing, but we didn't really like to talk about it much. She kept things under control, complained very little, and I didn't ask questions.

The decision to attempt to make a baby put us in a virtual bizarro-world. Kiersten would need to stop with the birth control, and we would thus enter into the unthinkable— we'd be miserable having sex. It wouldn't just cease being fun, it would *hurt*—and hurting my wife wasn't something I found particularly enjoyable—although it would have the twisted benefit of elation from my partner if I could muster up some premature ejaculation. When's the last time your wife asked if you were "done yet" before you could even start to focus in on interpretations of the infield fly rule, whether or not the initiative process is good for democracy, if there really are hidden messages on the Beatles' *White Album* if you play it backwards, or any of the other myriad things you think about to distract you from orgasm?

Gold star for under two minutes. Oh, the romance!

Just to be sure, however, we experimented with a couple of months off of the pill to see if she could handle it. It reminded me of an excruciating road trip to Reno my family took when I was ten—crammed in a 1981 diesel-engine Volkswagen Rabbit with nonstop hits of Anne Murray, Gordon Lightfoot, and Ronnie Milsap on cassette tape:

"Are we there yet?"

"No."

"Are we there yet?"

"No."

"Are we there yet?"

"NO!"

I might as well have been shoving a tire iron in there; without the hormones of the birth control pill, the poor girl couldn't get me off of her fast enough. Try as I might, the eroticism of my wife grimacing and gasping as if we were lovemaking in the middle of a septic tank made it virtually impossible for me to, ahem, "finish." It became clear that procreating on our own wasn't something that was likely without some kind of professional help.

As fate would have it, Kiersten's mother, Karen, had recently taken a position at a clinic specializing in helping couples in becoming pregnant. The clinic was small—a receptionist, a pair of nurses, a physician, and two embryologists, one being the wife of the main doc. This husband-and-wife team were family friends of sorts, as Kiersten often babysat their kids and we would frequently see them out on the town. We both knew what they did for a living, but neither of us could have imagined just how well we would get to know their business.

INDECENT PROPOSAL
(OCTOBER 2004)

It was approaching dusk and the sun bore through our lead-glass windows, highlighting the den in an array of crimson and scarlet as we moved into our respective positions for a relaxing evening of drinks and a Netflix movie we'd probably never remember. Kiersten sat on the couch, and I on the adjacent chair. Oddly, we rarely sat next to each other when we watched television. I always argued that it was because our couch was damned uncomfortable, but the jury was still out.

"Would you consider getting tested?" she said, somewhat out of the blue.

I'd guessed she was preoccupied by something, and Kiersten cut to the proverbial chase. I paused the movie, but poured my beer as I could sense I'd need it.

"IQ test? Myers-Briggs personality test? Breathalyzer test?" I cracked.

Do not pass go, do not collect $200 – my wit went in one ear and out the other. She was talking about an entirely different variety of testing, and I knew it.

"Well, this isn't going to be much fun...trying, that is...to have a baby."

"I know. I'm sorry."

We had recently been talking seriously about adding to our family above and beyond the quadruped variety. But we both knew we faced major obstacles.

I'd heard of the mundane routine of scheduled baby-making sex before—when the moment holds about as much personal meaning as brushing your dog's teeth. At this point, I was wishing we could be there, monitoring an ovulation calendar and hitting the hay for the specific purpose of procreation, as unromantic and tedious as it might be. Like normal people. Not like what I could sense was coming.

"I'm thinking maybe we can have your, um, *stuff* tested to make sure it will work if I'm going to have to be in so much pain to conceive," she said. "I want some level of confidence that it will work quickly."

"What would make you think that it wouldn't work?" I asked.

"Well, it's not like we've always been particularly safe."

Good point.

"And you know that I was a pill baby," she said.

"You can't tell me that your Mom took her pill religiously, though. I mean, I've seen your mother turn the ignition key in her car when it's already started."

"Well, my sister was an IUD baby! Explain that!" she said.

"Your mother is hyper fertile then, what does that explain?"

"You would think that I should be similar to her. We haven't even been safe and we haven't had any happy little mistakes."

"Maybe we shouldn't worry about something we don't know for sure."

"Well, have you always been safe with everyone else?" she asked.

"In the last month?" I ask.

Thank you folks, you've been a great crowd, I'll be here through Saturday...

"Michael!"

"Sorry . . . No, you're right," I relented. "What's your point?"

"And you've never impregnated anyone, right?"

That got my attention.

Shit. I guess I haven't. I always took that as a great accomplishment, but why does it strike me as particularly bad right now?

"So you need evidence? Would you like me to go impregnate someone?"

Dealing with stressful situations with humor was something that helped half the time and, during the other half, made Kiersten want to ensure I'd never have children with a swift kick to my groin. Her glare wasn't the typical "you smart ass, why couldn't I fall in love with someone more emotionally mature?" She was upset and scared. Frankly, so was I.

You're such a prick. Get serious, Michael...

"Okay, I'm in—anything for you," I said. "Make me an appointment, we'll see what's going on down there."

"Thank you," she said, "I'll ask my mom when they can get you in."

You'll ask your mom? What does your mom have to do with this?

I paused for a moment, bewildered. And then it hit me. *Oh... oh, no...*

At that moment, I have no doubt my look of unrelenting horror was overshadowed only by the loss of all the blood from my face. I might have even peed my pants, but I was numb from the shock, so how would I know? I imagine my expression was akin to that of the unfortunate character from *The Crying Game* when he realized his girlfriend had a penis (forgive me if you just queued that up in your Netflix account)

I'm going to have to jerk off in a cup about ten feet from my mother-in-law.

At that point, I left immediately to consult my therapist. She was from England, I think. Her name was Tanqueray and she visited me in a pretty green 150-mL bottle.

TAKING UP THE COLLECTION

My appointment was early—8:30 a.m. or so. I don't know if it was the early hour or not, but I swear, when I walked in that office, the lights were dimmed.

This is some kind of sick joke, isn't it? They've actually given me fucking mood lighting? Where's the Barry White?

The office itself did not inspire spontaneous erotic notions. It boasted standard issue green and puce carpet and veneer wood chairs with flotation-device-like cushions— great for a flood but not really for waiting. The walls displayed a smattering of framed accolades which the office had received and publications in which the good doctor had been featured. In many of the photographs, he was holding little vials of God-knows-what or gesturing to some piece of machinery or a smiling pair of clients.

I looked them over and subsequently assigned new headlines to each of them:

"Man Makes Good on Boyhood Promise to Pay Men for Masturbating"

"Babies Made by Doctor Using Gum, Erector Set, and Elbow Grease"

"Physician Delivers Twelfth Cloned Self"

There wasn't much movement, so I made my way towards the back of the office, looking for Ken, the embryologist.

Ken was the kind of guy on whom you rarely found any expression but a smile. Always jovial, professional, and a glass-half-full kind of guy, Ken had the gleam in his eye and the manicured beard of a caricature Irish leprechaun, except much taller. And, hopefully, his area of expertise was fertility treatment rather than general mischief and pot-o-gold tending.

"Hey, Michael—there you are. Are you early?" Ken asked.

Why…is this romantic lighting for you and the zillion sperm back here?

"Am I?"

"Well, I guess it doesn't matter—we don't have any other appointments this morning… at least I don't think so…"

You don't think so? Wonderful, I can just envision an impatient line of would-be "donators" tapping their feet and anxiously checking their watches outside the collection room door. Could you play the 'Jeopardy' theme music while I'm in there too? "I'll take 'Things you'd rather die than do in the same building with your mother-in-law' for $500…"

"Here's everything you need, just be sure to read the instructions."

Oh man, I seriously can't wait to see the instructions…

"Put the lid on the sample nice and tight, put it back in the bag and place it here when you're finished." He gestured toward a ceramic tray, which upon further inspection, revealed itself to be a brownish colored hot plate with little white designs fired right into it. I felt fairly confident what they were, but I couldn't resist asking. "Ummm, Ken—is this a hot plate?"

"Yeah."

"Are there sperm on your hot plate?"

"Yep. Neat, huh?"

"And, I put my can of sperm on the 'sperm hot plate,' correct?"

"Yes."

Ah, of course—for all those well functioning monkeys you're treating, right? Does Bobo get a carrot after he does his business?

Putting the hot-plate incident aside, I located the collection room, and with my brown paper bag, instructions, and cup neatly tucked inside, I entered, shut the door, and audibly clicked the lock three or four times until it sounded extra-locked.

"Let the party begin," I muttered.

Off-white imitation-tile linoleum covered the floor. I saw a sink, a mirror, a toilet, and a fluffy couch covered in a white sheet. Vegas, this was not.

Whatever you do, don't think about how many hairy-assed men have smacked their sausage on that couch. Ugh...I just did it. Arrrgh...I just did it again...

Upon further inspection, I noticed a bin full of magazines which immediately piqued my interest. On the wall was a simple round clock with a black frame.

A clock? Was I supposed to punch in? Am I paying hourly in here? Aren't minutes free before 9:00 or something?

The couch continued to give me the heebie-jeebies, so I sat on the toilet, anxious to read my instructions.

These better not say I have to use my left hand — I'll be in here until 2:30.

I pulled out the instruction sheet and the semen receptacle, which appeared to be about a quart large, fit for mixing paint.

If I have to fill this thing up, I'm going to need a case of KY and a pack of smokes...

"This cup will hold what may be a small sample of your semen," read the instructions.

Whew.

"It is designed to ensure we get as much of the sample inside as possible."

Inside? As opposed to what?

I immediately scanned the floor.

All clear...

"Please record the time you ejaculate."

Ah, the mystery of the clock is solved.

"Please make a note of any semen that does not make it inside the cup and if it was lost when you first ejaculated, during, or toward the end."

Lost?! Again, I scan the floor. They could really use a black floor in here.

"Okay, let's get this over with," I sighed.

I'm a man who believes that if God didn't intend for us to masturbate, he'd have given us tiny, Tyrannosaurus-Rex-like arms, and certainly wouldn't have blessed us with opposable thumbs. Nevertheless, I was amazed to discover just how challenging this endeavor was to become.

Setting aside my fears of the fluffy couch, I knew nothing magical was going to take place either standing or on that uncomfortable damned toilet, so I unbuckled my jeans, dropped my drawers and planted my ass on the sofa. Looking down wearily, I noted that nothing much was happening.

I need inspiration…

The magazine selection could provide a couple of chapters on its own—but suffice to say these magazines were clearly not chosen by anyone remotely close to a porn connoisseur. They were visibly worn and none of them were from this millennium.

They've worked for thousands before me, so why be choosy…

Logistically, imagine my dilemma: cup in one hand, appendage in the other.

I need someone to turn the pages for me…where's the stewardess call button?

Don't get me wrong, the singular lovely young lady I had landed upon from April of 1993 wasn't hurting my situation, but if you fixate on the same motionless vagina for an extended period of time, it begins to lose its allure… kind of in the same way that if you say the word "boob" enough times, it begins to sound nonsensical.

I can't stare at this AquaNet spokesperson in that pose for another second.

I dropped the cup and risked it, and immediately realized why the instructions asked you to try and get as much of the "sample" in the cup as possible. Undoubtedly, the staff had product-tested this room—they knew you had to turn the magazine pages for full effect. Impressed, I carried on with the task at, and in, hand.

With my porn quandary solved, I sampled the variety while marveling at my multi-tasking ability. Things were going swimmingly, and I anticipated I'd be finishing up any moment now when I noticed a pair of feet walk up to the base of the door, stop just for a nanosecond, and then walk away.

Whaaaaa…What the fuck just happened? Could that have been my mother-in-law? Do you think she heard anything?

Oh. My. God.

No.

No…

NO!

This is a nightmare.

Wake up.

Wake up.

Not working…

Not working…

Still half naked in this antiseptic room with crappy porn and a cup to jerk off in and my mother-in-law might be outside the door.

I could hear Howard Cosell in my head, "Down goes Frazier! Down goes Frazier! Down goes Frazier!"

Back to square one.

This is ridiculous.

I decided I needed a change of scenery. I relocated to the edge of the couch, facing as far away from the door as possible and shuffled through the "visual aids," deciding on another late-nineties erotic gem who had without a doubt satisfied numerous men across the country who started each sentence with the word "dude."

I'm proud to report my mission was back on track in no time. Page after page of mildly attractive women, who were probably now nearing the age of 40, selflessly attended to my visual erotic needs.

...cup...where did I leave the cup . . .

Shit.

SHIT.

During my migration from one end of the couch to the other, I hadn't packed my bags appropriately and left the cup out of arm's reach.

I stood, pants around my ankles, shuffled my feet like a prisoner ball-and-chained, grabbed my cup and resumed my seat on the end of the couch.

God is laughing at me, I just know it.

Gazing southward intently, I honestly had a telepathic conversation with my penis:

You can do this. I know you can. I've seen you do this a thousand times before. I know these are strange surroundings. I know my brain is sending you strange signals. But we can get through this together. Now make me proud.

Newly motivated, we endeavored to complete our duty.

The cup was clearly in view.

My left-handed page-turning skill was unparalleled.

The finish line was near.

And then...

Geena Davis? Is that THE Geena Davis... topless?

Please understand I mean no disrespect to the very lovely Ms. Davis, but the last thing I expected to see was a 12-year-old picture of an extremely skinny and freckled screen actress who most definitely did not possess the kind of, uh... *attributes* the other young women boasted in this oh-so-classy publication.

What's worse, not only were Geena Davis and her bare breasts (which bore no similarities to any of the other pairs throughout the magazine, with the exception of their physical location) burning holes in my eyes, but the man sitting next to her was wearing a tiny...black...Speedo.

Turn the page! Left hand, GO!

My eyes!

The horror!

...happy place, happy place, happy place...

"I've got to get my own visual aids next time," I groused.

Although I discarded the Geena Davis boardwalk top-less extravaganza and selected a new dirty rag, visions of the scene from *The Fly* where she plucked that disgusting coarse hair out of Jeff Goldblum's back haunted me.

Nevertheless, my business with the cup, the clock, the couch that couldn't believe how its life had turned out, the sub-par adult magazines, and my beleaguered right hand pressed on.

Minutes later, my preposterous little affair ended.

Lid tightly fixed, I scribbled out the time on my instruction sheet. "Okay...9:07. All of the sample..."

I scanned the floor.

"...made it in the cup."

Exiting the collection room, I noticed the white sheet that once neatly covered the couch now appeared to have endured a battle between two rhinoceros in heat.

Hmm...should I make up that couch before I leave or should I just get the hell out of here?

I heard some chatting from the back room and panicked. What would someone say to me if they saw me standing in front of that collection room door, holding my paper bag and staring at the war-torn couch?

"So, how did it go in there?"

"Everything come out okay?"

"Did you lose any of the sample?"

"Did you see Geena Davis?"

My choice was clear—I needed to get out of there. I hung an immediate left, located the "sperm hot plate," dropped off my bag o' fun, and headed back down the hallway to make an unceremonious exit.

Arriving at the lobby, I noticed two couples waiting in their floatation-device-chairs, oblivious to how well equipped they were for a tsunami. I hadn't adequately prepared for this part of my departure—it was something completely unexpected. Each of them looked at me as if I had a massive cold sore on my face, my fly was open, or perhaps I was performing as a mime…that half-smiling, eyebrows-raised, forehead-wrinkled, I-see-you-but-please-don't-come-near-me gaze.

They know.

"Hi, I'm Michael—I just masturbated back there. It's nice to meet you. Is this your wife? Hi there, I just 'punched the clown' in that room over there. Yeah, good times, good times. Have you seen the sperm hot plate? It's a pleasure to meet you…"

Dear Ken, it's 9:12 a.m. —and all of my dignity made it into the cup.

*A father's pride, laid on thick, has always
made me wish that the fellow had at least
experienced some pain during procreation.*

– Karl Krauss (1874-1936)

DECISIONS

You already know the outcome of the semen analysis: sperm count was average, motility wasn't great, morphology was worse. But there were apparently enough decent boys in there that Dr. Granderson thought we were good candidates for In Vitro Fertilization (IVF). While the news about my 'boys' was far from ideal, at least we knew what we were up against, and we had someone with lots of education and an affinity for big words I didn't understand who thought he could help us…and that had to be considered a good thing at this point.

Feeling like this was something I should have asked *before* my marathon session in the collection room, I threw him the first softball question to get our latest meeting started.

"So what's involved—I… I don't even know what in-vitro is. I just think of a Petri dish and a turkey baster."

Granderson sat up proudly, almost excitedly, and began to gesture wildly with his hands. You could tell he took great joy in his job. He spoke methodically, with a baritone monochromatic drawl and a penchant for placing emphasis on the last word of each sentence. His vocal cadence put a smile on my face, despite the subject matter.

"Basically we control Kiersten's period with birth control pills and then give her a variety of hormones to produce as many healthy eggs as we can."

Oh, goody—hormone roller coaster ahead. How many tickets for this ride?

"Then we extract the eggs and fertilize them with your semen…"

I immediately checked behind me, just to make sure…yep, he was talking to me. Phew.

"…either through a more natural fertilization process where we essentially dump your semen on top of her eggs, or through a process where we actually choose healthy sperm and inject it into the egg with a very small needle."

For good measure, he drew us a picture. Of course, another world-class circle.

Show-off.

"Once we determine the egg is fertilized, we choose the ones that we think have the best chance of implanting and we put them in Kiersten's uterus using a specialized catheter."

My ears rang.

"You just said 'ones'… You choose the *ones*, as in plural?"

Granderson nodded and tightened his lips, almost as if he was avoiding laughing at me.

"We like to maximize the possibility of implantation by inserting multiple fertilized eggs."

I swallowed. I swallowed hard.

Kiersten took over. "Does my age affect the number of eggs you put in?"

"Absolutely. Very good question."

How come I feel like I'm developmentally delayed over here? Just give me a coloring book and some crayons and carry on with your adult conversation...

"For a woman in her early twenties, we might only put two eggs in. For a woman in her late twenties to early thirties, we might put in three. For someone in their late thirties to early forties, we can put in more—but not enough to make a basketball team..."

God love him for taking a stab at humor, but this was delivered as if it had been said 8,000 times before. But he was so likable and sincere, we both gave him a genuine courtesy laugh.

"How do the rates of pregnancy vary with the number of eggs implanted?" Kiersten asked.

"If we implant two, there's about a 30 percent chance of pregnancy. If we implant three, there's about a 40 percent chance."

"And multiples?" she asked.

"With two eggs, the twin rates are very low, in the teens. With three eggs, there's about a 25 percent chance of twins and about a two to three percent chance of triplets."

I might have gotten up and walked out if he had mentioned quadruplets.

"And what happens to the fertilized eggs that don't get used?" Kiersten asked.

"They are cryogenically frozen," Granderson replied.

Pause.

"Is that to repopulate the Earth after nuclear war?" I asked.

Kiersten turned to me and said, "It's for us to use if the first round doesn't work."

I am two feet tall.

Granderson broke the subsequent uncomfortable silence, "Well, this gives you guys something to think about. I'm confident we can get you a baby if you decide to do this, and I hope you do. Do you have any more questions?"

Had I opened my mouth, I'm fairly sure Granderson's pencil would have been firmly planted in my neck—a parting gift from my wife for my display of ignorance and emotional immaturity.

I smiled.

No questions here. I really just wanted to know if it was still happy hour at my favorite pub. I felt a strong urge to suggest we go to the brewery so we could decompress over a half dozen well crafted brews, but I had a sense the timing wasn't quite right for guzzling inebriants.

We thanked Granderson for his time and exited upwards to the parking lot from his basement office, clanging up the metal stairs which echoed with an industrial resonance fit for a prison.

Kiersten was noticeably quiet. I playfully grabbed her hips on the way up, partly because I just loved her shape and partly because I was trying to lighten her spirits. She shook free, wordless.

Am I in trouble? I wondered.

Reaching the car, I noticed a sign in front of the Chevy Yukon next to us that read "Parking for limited mobility patients."

"Honey, they should have a spot for limited motility patients!" I said.

No reaction.

"Get it?"

She was just waiting for me to unlock the car.

Well, damn, I thought that was actually pretty funny.

I had either underestimated how badly Kiersten wanted a baby or how emotional the previous conversation with Granderson had been for her, or both. She broke down as soon as we pulled away from the clinic and sobbed uncontrollably.

I knew this wasn't my strength. I'd never been particularly good at the consoling husband role—I usually analyzed and tried to fix instead of just shutting up and offering a hug. I'm sure that's in the Mars and Venus book somewhere.

Seeing as how I was driving, I just chose to shut up.

Twelve Kleenex and a few minutes later, she asked, "Aren't you at all upset?!"

Trick question. I know there's a good answer inside you, I just know it.

"About what?"

Great response, Dr. Phil.

"ABOUT THE FACT THAT WE CAN'T HAVE KIDS!"

"I thought we just heard that we can?"

In my defense, I really believed that. For some reason, I wasn't as affected by this as I probably ought to have been. In my mind, we had just been spared a year of trying and failing. We had a path to take to conceiving a child, it just wasn't the one we would have chosen.

Kiersten didn't process that way. I should have known better.

"No, we heard that we CAN'T MAKE BABIES ON OUR OWN. We heard that I've got to get poked and prodded and GO THROUGH HELL FOR A FUCKING 30 PERCENT CHANCE THAT IT WORKS."

"Okay, calm down…" I said.

Now, one of the most sacred rules regarding the order of the universe is that when men say "calm down" to their wives, it happens exactly .0034% of the time. Trust me, I've looked it up. Science doesn't lie.

"DON'T TELL ME TO CALM DOWN! I can't believe that you're not upset by this!"

I started taking inventory of my liquor cabinet at home.

I'm pretty sure I have at least half a bottle of Makers Mark and enough Tanqueray for a martini. That should get me through the evening. I need olives though…hmm…seems like a bad time to stop…

I reverted back to 'shut up' mode despite what was probably both of our desires that I find the right thing to say. But what was the right thing to say?

"It's okay, Doc will make us something nice" seemed insensitive.

"30% chance is better odds than the Mariners winning the pennant" would just piss her off.

"There's always eBay" was just plain stupid.

They don't make greeting cards for these kinds of occasions.

There was little I could do.

I hated to see her so upset, but all I could think of was to keep driving and try to avoid saying the wrong thing.

Of children as of procreation —
the pleasure momentary,
the posture ridiculous,
the expense damnable.

– Evelyn Waugh (1903-1966)

Pickles and Bottoms

O ur situation was far from the romantic ideal of baby-making. I'm sure Kiersten had some kind of idyllic fantasy about the process of growing our family, about the night the baby was conceived, how she just "knew" she was pregnant afterwards, and being able to share all the details with friends thereafter. This wasn't terribly likely anymore. And beyond the basic injury was an added in-sult—our current predicament had the aggravating impact of ruining my Christmas present to Kiersten.

We started having serious discussions about a baby around September or October, which was a couple months before Granderson, collection rooms, shameful pictures of celebrities, and all of this in-vitro nonsense came to be. That's when my education about "baby stuff" began. The options when it came to crap you could buy for your kid were sim-ply dizzying. Cribs, changing tables, bedding, strollers, joggers, car seats, humidifiers, diaper genies, room decora-tions, baby swings, white noise machines, and the toys, my God, the toys! The list was no doubt endless. Somewhere, that cursed little Geoffrey the giraffe from 'Toys R Us' was grinning greedily and rubbing his hooves together.

One of the items you apparently needed was a diaper bag. I soon learned that in order to be a "hip" mother, you needed a diaper bag that looked more like a chi-chi hand-bag than a place to store expensive sponges for your kid's excrement. Given all the ways we positively spin the gross and disgusting, I'm still a little befuddled at why these are called 'diaper bags' instead of 'cherub carry-all' or 'little angel attaché' or maybe even 'mama tote.' Regardless, Kiersten had already arrived at a decision on who would make her diaper bag; she was just trying to decide between models.

The brand, much to my amazement, was called "Petunia Picklebottom." The company tended to name their bags much the same way chic paint makers named their colors: *Green Tea, Spring Roll, Fortune Cookie,* and so on. One bag name was "Fond of Flora." This was a particularly appropriate bag name since it was currently the favored name for a girl on Kiersten's long, long, painfully long, list of baby names. It was also the design that she liked the most, which, let's just get down to brass tacks, was the most important part. The damned bag could be called 'Hitler's Haversack' as long as it was the design she wanted. The biggest problem was the prohibitive price tag—apparently Ms. Picklebottom drove a PickleLexus. It was an expense that she wasn't willing to incur just yet.

Much to Kiersten's ultimate surprise, I do listen to her, even when my mind appears to be in outer space. I wrote the name of that overpriced rucksack and the bizarre name of the bag maker down and put it in a safe place. It would make an excellent gift, I figured. For the next several weeks, I scoured every possible place in town that carried these lovely little reservoirs for formula, pacifiers, and wipes, but nobody seemed to carry "Fond of Flora."

I decided to venture online. After a short search, I had a list of stores which carried Petunia Picklebottom bags, and I made my way down about half of that list, calling each vendor, before I found someone with one last "Fond of Flora" bag. I didn't even bother asking what they wanted for it; I just said to box it up and send it.

That's about the time we sat down with Dr. Granderson to discover that we are to baby making what Michael Jordan was to the game of baseball—a tragically bad match. So there I was with a baby diaper bag, which I assumed would arrive lined in pure gold with a diamond studded buckle, and the small detail of not being able to actually make a baby. My Dad would call that "all dressed up and no date."

So what the hell was I to do? I could go buy something else and just have the bag kicking around in case we ever needed it. I could just give it to her and show her my commitment to seeing this process through.

I considered the possible reactions. On the one hand, she could think it was the sweetest thing in the world and I would be rewarded with an evening of steamy hot-tub action that would make Snooki from *Jersey Shore* proud. On the other hand, she could open it and break down, berating me for buying such an insensitive gift, and I'd end up spending the night on the couch where Bella, my bulldog, would pass gas in my face every hour, on the hour in an act of solidarity with the woman of the house.

I decided to risk it. I gave it to her.

Fortunately, she was genuinely excited to see what was hidden behind my sorry excuse for a wrapping job. She was cognizant of what it represented, though—filling this thing with baby crap wouldn't be the hard part. Having a reason to fill it with baby crap would be. As such, I think she was just a little bit sad when she saw it. But overall, it was well received.

It didn't go over perfectly, however. Despite the warm reception, Kiersten's high-class, handmade, priced-for-someone-who-makes-a-whole-lot-more-than-I-do diaper bag was placed into a dark corner where she didn't want to see it again until it was ready to be used. No baby, no bag.

I started to harbor ill will towards this elegantly embroidered Huggies tote. Every time I'd happen upon it, I'd rather petulantly say the same thing.

"What are *you* looking at, Petunia Picklebottom?"

I hoped that it would be dusted off sooner rather than later.

FOOD FOR THOUGHT

Kiersten and I were impulse buyers. We bought our first car together after one test drive. We bought our first house with a full-price offer even though we could scarcely recall all the details of the house after we saw it. What's the holdup? We saw, we liked, we went home with it.

Over the next few weeks, we talked. I mean, we *really* communicated. This was to be our most difficult decision together to date. There was no impulse in-vitro. As always, we did our best thinking when we were eating— preferably without involving our own kitchen and ideally somewhere with menus and a wait staff.

"So we're still planning on adopting, right?" she asked, hunching over her cornmeal pancakes.

"What breed?"

Blank stare.

"Yes, of course. It's in 'The Plan', right?"

"I think if we did adopt," she said, "we should do it in-ternationally."

"Agreed. What did you have in mind?" I stabbed at my oatmeal with my fork, trying to resist the impulse to fling a glob of it at the woman in the table next to me who couldn't stop blathering on about stopping "the Taliban on her block."

"China," she said definitively.

"China," I said, in more of an echo than a question.

"What's wrong with China?"

"I'm not sure that you could name a little Asian baby Clementine or Astrid, honey."

She crinkled her nose at me.

I grinned and took stock of my oatmeal, wondering if they had actually brought me granola instead. Was there a practical difference other than the temperature, I wondered.

"Did I ever tell you how I wanted to adopt from China going all the way back to high school?" I asked her.

"Seriously?" Kiersten had a look that was waiting for a punch line.

"Yeah. I don't know why I never said anything about it earlier. But when I first heard about the population issues in China and how that orphaned thousands of girls, I thought it was something I should do. I even recall watching my parents roll their eyes at me when I first mentioned it, although who could blame them—I couldn't even operate an iron and could barely microwave a bowl of soup at 18."

"Don't you think that's weird?" she asked.

"What's weird?"

"That we both have always wanted to adopt, and we both prefer China."

"Yeah, I suppose it is."

"We're meant to be together," she said.

"Well I'm glad you've finally come to that conclusion after seven years of marriage."

"Why haven't you mentioned it before?" she asked.

"I think I was always a little scared, felt too immature to do something so important."

"Scared of what?"

"Issues of trying to integrate an appropriate mix of their ethnic culture while raising them. Issues of wanting to meet their biological parents. 'You can't tell me what to do, you're not my real Dad'... that kind of scared."

"You don't give yourself enough credit," she said.

"How so?"

"You would deal with all of that just fine. You'll be a great father."

She started to cry.

Okay, don't say anything stupid. Umm...hold her hand! Hold her hand! That's got to be good!

I reached across and took her hand and didn't say a thing.

She smiled.

The waterworks eased.

Bingo.

"I know I want to adopt, but..." she said.

"But what?"

"...but I know I want one that looks like you," she said dejectedly.

"You know I'm not Asian, right?"

"Michael..."

"Sorry."

"I think I want a baby that is biological first. One that looks like you, then we can adopt," she reiterated.

"So if it comes out and it looks like the neighbor, do we have to try again?"

No response.

"Okay, well, wasn't a bio baby and an adopted baby always part of 'The Plan'?"

"I suppose so," she acquiesced.

I decided to state the obvious. "Well that clearly narrows down our options, huh?"

"I suppose it does."

Making my case, I posited, "If trying to have a kid the old fashioned way is going to be a living hell, and if adoption is what we want after a biological kid, our decision is pretty much made, isn't it?"

She fiddled with the few remaining blueberries from her breakfast, staring into her plate. "It's just so hard, you know—to consciously make the decision to terrorize your body. I wish someone could make up our minds for us, could just say, 'Look, this is what you have to do to have a kid and it's guaranteed it will work,' or if there was some kind of divine intervention, a clear celestial sign that would show us whether or not to do IVF..."

A waitress approached the table. "More coffee?"

"Do these cups come in larger sizes?" I cracked.

Ignoring me, she refilled my cup, splashing a little on my hand as she pulled the pot back. Hating to waste any caffeine, I lapped it up like a sloppy dog.

The restaurant was cozy, with tightly packed tables sparing enough room for people to scoot through sideways. As our waitress topped off our coffee, a woman backed up behind her on her way out.

"Excuse me," said the anonymous woman to our waitress. "Come on, kids—say goodbye to the nice lady, we're leaving."

She slowly shuffled past our table with roughly four-month-old twins.

We stared at them.

They stared at us.

We stared at each other.

"Do you want me to call the clinic or would you like to?" I said.

BLACK TUESDAY

My wife is a teacher. As such, she is a planner (we like to say "planner" instead of "control freak" around these parts). The whole timeline for having a baby had to fall within a certain window of acceptable months. The baby couldn't come in the summer, because she needed to start the school year in order for her medical benefits to kick in. The baby couldn't come in the fall because she would have to go back to work in the spring in order for us to manage financially. The baby couldn't come in December because that's when Kiersten's birthday was and according to Kiersten, there was nothing more traumatizing than having a December birthday because you inevitably get ripped off on the whole birthday party and presents front due to, in her words, "competing holidays." Don't laugh, she'll hear you. Honestly, on this subject, I've learned not to dare argue with those born under the ninth sign of the zodiac (Sagittarius). Yeesh!

We conferred with the clinic to see when they had available cycles. They could get us in late March. I started counting on my fingers as I ran through the months, "March, April, May…"

Kiersten not-so-delicately put the kibosh on that idea, "No way, that's a December baby waiting to happen. What about late May or June?"

Sold.

We were penciled in in five months' time. There was no turning back.

All that was left was a consultation with Susan, one of the clinic's nurses, who was in charge of giving us a general idea of what to expect when the process started in a few months, as well as instructions for some rumored "lifestyle changes" that I needed to hear about. I figured I'd have to drink more water and maybe hop on a treadmill occasionally, but I soon discovered I couldn't have been more wrong.

Susan had olive skin and raven-black hair which she pulled back tightly in a bun. She had the general appearance of one of those Robert Palmer dancers in the "Addicted to Love" video, sans the bean-pole figure. When delivering information, Susan liked to end her sentences with "okay?" For the next forty-five minutes, I'd be thinking:

No, that's not okay.

No, not okay.

No.

No.

No.

But I digress...

She tended to smile a lot—even when she was delivering information that was especially distressing. As personal characteristics go, it was unnerving. I couldn't help wondering how she looked when she read the Monday obituaries.

"Why are you so happy, Susan?"
"Oh, just the dead people..."

Susan began our meeting by slapping her hands on both knees and smiling from ear to ear. I swear to God I thought she was going to start a cheer.

"Ready? Okay!"

"I'm going to talk to you guys today about your calendar, okay? When we're done with that, I'm going to talk to you, Michael, about some do's and don'ts over the next five months, okay? I'm afraid you might not like me much when we're done."

Funny...I don't like you much already.

She spent the next twenty minutes describing when the hormone injections (yes, I said injections, but we'll get to that later) started for Kiersten, when the "retrieval" (taking the eggs out) and when the "transfer" (putting the fertilized eggs back in) were scheduled. This was all neatly organized on a calendar which she subsequently handed us.

"Take some time to look it over and let me know if you have any questions, okay?"

Kiersten inspected the calendar with great consideration. She ran down each week with her index finger. I could almost hear the gears cranking in her head as she calculated how this calendar would work with her teaching schedule. Better yet—she was checking for errors. I just loved it when she did other people's jobs better than they did.

I glanced at the calendar. I didn't really bother to read it, but I wanted to at least pretend I cared enough to look it over—kind of like when they asked you to sample the bottle of wine at a restaurant. So I smelled the cork, I breathed in the aroma, I swirled it around, I sipped, and then looked intrigued…

The majority of this calendar has to do with Kiersten and I knew she was going to have it memorized backwards and forwards by the time we get home today. But a particular day among the myriad of injections, ultrasounds, extractions, and retrievals caught my attention. In bold capital letters, there was a day that I was surely going to appreciate: "MICHAEL MUST EJACULATE."

"Hey, that day looks like fun!" I proclaimed with post-pubescent glee.

Kiersten gave me a glance that almost assured me that I'd be enjoying that date on my own.

"It's actually important that you ejaculate at least every two to three days over the next five months—especially in the last couple of months, okay?" Susan instructed.

Susan for President! Viva Susan!

"After the date when you must ejaculate, it's really critical that you not ejaculate for the next six days thereafter, okay?"

Evil, foul temptress…

"Now to maximize the strength of your sperm, you're going to need to cut back on the alcohol and coffee, okay?"

Beginning to get the shakes, I queried, "Define 'cutting back'."

*   *   *

Allow me to provide some context. My drinks of choice were typically gin (dry), bourbon (neat), red wine (the fuller the better), and beer (a well done Imperial IPA could nearly bring me to tears…if I had four, then fully to tears.). I didn't drink solely because of the effects of alcohol; I chose these particular drinks because I truly loved their flavor. I get a nostalgic, fuzzy sensation just writing about them, as if they were old friends.

I was a firm believer that drinks ought to make one grimace. A good drink should hurt. A watered-down martini was a colossal waste of time and liquor. A glass of Maker's full of ice all too quickly became a glass of water with some Makers. Others committed far worse offenses, of course. Pouring 7-Up in your glass of Tanqueray or 'flavoring' your Makers Mark with Pepsi was like painting over 100-year-old clear vertical-grain fir floors in Martha Stewart Robin's Egg Blue. People ought to be put down for certain crimes against good taste.

I was similar with my coffee. I liked it strong…very strong. And I liked it to taste like…hold on to your hat…*coffee.* I'd pass on the flavoring. No caramel muck-it-uppos or whatever they're called. An eggnog latte should require a sin tax. A 'mocha' wasn't a coffee drink, it was dessert with a splash of caffeine. My drink of choice was a quad shot of espresso with a little bit of hot water. Yummy.

On both fronts, spirits and coffee that is, I subscribed to the modus vivendi that a good friend of mine once revealed to me whilst in an easy chair with a fine craft brew in hand. "Michael," he said, looking distantly at the wall, almost as if it were transparent and he was finally realizing total consciousness, "…drinking in moderation is just stupid."

A typical week included a few trips to watering holes after work with friends, featuring a couple beers, perhaps three. Kiersten and I would also have a pair of dates out which always involved a couple of glasses of wine highlighted by innocent flirtations. It was rare for me to get home and unwind without a drink or two, whether or not I had just returned from a bar where I was unwinding with a drink or two. There was a cathartic effect gleaned from mixing a drink and sipping it slowly, be it the gin martini up with olives or Makers neat (maybe a small cube to cool it off…).

Weekends were another story. If a Friday night or Saturday event was planned with a group of friends, it often got ugly, frequently resulting in the need for copious acetaminophen and Gatorade the next morning.

Coffee was consumed like the addict I was. A quad Americano from my dealer on my walk to work, another double short Americano by 2:00 to get me to quitting time, and then it wasn't uncommon to consume another double or triple shot as a treat with my lady friend. I loved coffee and coffee loved me. I knew it did. It told me so. If you know otherwise, don't tell me, it will break my heart.

This, I would soon learn, partially explained the subpar semen analysis. For the week prior to the "collection," I had been on a veritable bender, epitomized by roughly three gin martinis, two glasses of Pinot Noir, and a beer the night before the actual deposit. Thank goodness I had great quantities of espresso to snap me back each day.

*   *   *

"Define 'cutting back'."

"Well, in the three months prior to your collection date, you're allowed eight ounces of red wine a night, but no beer at all, okay?"

"I'm sorry, were you speaking to me?" I stuttered.

"Yes," Susan said with a grand smile on her face.

"...right, right...um...and I thought you just said 'no beer' but you must have said something else like 'go beer' or 'mo beer'..."

My expertise at killing brain cells was so cleverly masked.

Susan relented. "Well, technically you can have two per week, okay?"

Excellent... if I can continue to wear her down, I'll be up to 12 in no time...

"Two beers. Like two 12-ounce beers?"

"Mm-hmm," she hummed, in an intonation that clearly conveyed the unuttered "okay."

"What kind of beer? Are we talking domestic two-percent alcohol beer or two 11 percent alcohol imperial IPA's?"

"I'd say avoid high-alcohol beers altogether, but feel free to have a micro-brew if you need to, okay?"

If I need to? I'm visibly sweating, aren't I?

I could feel Kiersten looking at me and smiling—wincing perhaps—like the look parents give their kids when they finally tell them there's no Santa Claus. Either that or she was just impressed I had taken such an interest in the process and was finally asking detailed questions.

"You mentioned something about coffee," I spouted, figuring the worst news had already come.

"Right, you need to stop drinking caffeine altogether, okay?"

I almost killed her, right then and there.

Um, no...not okay.

"You can have decaf coffee if you'd like, okay?"

Um, no...not okay.

I sensed my withdrawal symptoms beginning already.

Before we finished, Susan reached into her bag of rules and found a tidy little dagger. "Oh, and before I let you go—I didn't mention anything about liquor, but I figure that goes without saying... you can't have any liquor whatsoever, okay?"

Images of William Shatner in classic Star Trek over-acting tempo hit me...

Doc...what...will...become...of...me...?

*I drink too much, way too much. I gave my Doc
a urine sample and there was an olive in it.*

- Rodney Dangerfield

HURRY UP AND WAIT

For the next two months, I was hyper-diligent in my efforts to create and accept each and every opportunity to have a drink or a robust cup of coffee. It was a wondrous distraction from this miserable gloom that haunted me, this magnificent secret that I refused to share with anyone, even my family. I'd tell you more about all of my drinking escapades during that time, but frankly, I don't remember it terribly well. Go figure.

Now fully understanding the notion that time flies when you're having fun, I came to the abrupt end of my two months and was, for all practical purposes, on the wagon. Curbing the alcohol intake really wasn't much of an issue until we went out with friends who knew my penchant for a potent potable. After a glass of wine, I'd switch to decaf coffee, maybe a root beer, or perhaps just stick with water, which resulted in some particularly interesting looks. For many friends, it would have seemed more normal for me to drop my pants, stand on a chair, stick my finger in my nose and start singing "I'm a Yankee Doodle Dandy" than it would for me to shut down after one drink. Suddenly, going out to a bar was not only a waste of my time, but an immense burden. How was I going to fool everyone for the next three months?

With a certain group of friends, I could get away with the occasional "not feeling well" or "I have an important presentation tomorrow morning and I want to stay sharp" excuse. But for a couple of closer friends, I had to come up with some kind of rationale. Otherwise, it was just downright eerie for them to hang out with me. Our conversations tended to go like this:

"Want to shoot another game of pool?" I asked.

"I'm in—you rack, I'll get us more beer. What are you drinking?"

"No, I'm good. Coke is fine."

"Fuck you, what are you drinking?"

"No, really, I'm fine—not feeling well."

"Shut up. I'm bringing you whatever is on special, then."

Wonderful.

Too many times, I begged total strangers to drink my beer while my friends went to the bathroom. While I seemed to make a lot of new friends this way, it wasn't a solution that could last.

So I just blamed my dry spell on some nebulous, undefined "health" issue, explaining that the Doc said I needed to cut back. I'd fend off specific questions now and again, but by and large, it worked. I figured it really only needed to hold up for three months, then I'd have a miraculous recovery and the libations would flow freely!

One problem I hadn't foreseen was school. I was finishing up my Master's degree, and as such, I was writing my thesis. Now I'm no Hemmingway, but I certainly understood where the guy was coming from when he argued that he wrote his best stuff sauced. The majority of my thesis was written with the blood of grapes and hops all over it, and attempting to put the finishing touches on it with green tea was just not doing it for me. But this was a thesis, after all, which we all know doubles as insomnia therapy. I knew I could power through.

Surrendering my coffee habit was surprisingly painful. I complained about the taste of decaf for about the first week until I realized my discriminating buds were the least of my concerns with regard to persona non grata beverage #2. First came the headaches—the heavy, oppressive, eternal headaches. They lasted for approximately three or four days and then mellowed into a general splinter-in-my-skull kind of annoyance.

Following the headaches was something that I have a hard time explaining. It went on for roughly two weeks. I had a full-body physical reaction, which could only be described as something between debilitating exhaustion and quasi-depression. I felt like my body had been used by the New York Giants offensive linemen as the tackling dummy and then I was verbally abused by Chris Matthews on *Hardball*. I was a complete and utter feeble wreck.

Realistically, I had expected some kind of withdrawal. I wasn't kidding myself going into this—I knew I was the guy who started asking all of the baristas across town in early December whether or not they would be open on Christmas day. Only looking back at it now do I realize I was basically a yuppie version of Dave Chappelle's crack addict persona, Tyrone Biggums. Instead of a glass pipe, I used a paper cup with inspirational haikus printed on the side.

I became one with decaf in time, however. And later learning that there's still a hint of caffeine in decaf made me feel strangely content, like I wasn't turning my back on a longtime compatriot. *You're in there somewhere,* I figured. If anything, the brief respite from mightily caffeinated beverages only made me more excited for the day when I could quaff a quad espresso, gingerly sipping the bubbly caramel colored crème that lay delicately on top of the brewed gold beneath.

These three months also acted as an unexpected vetting period for our friends and acquaintances. We ultimately did share our circumstances with select friends, but had you asked us six months prior with whom we would share our deepest secrets, the list would have featured very different names. There was something about the very personal and delicate nature of our situation which made us quite fastidious about whom we told. As a result, we both felt we had created a much closer, more robust bond with certain friends. Ultimately, these were the people who we thought could be supportive as well as discreet, and they certainly helped us get through this agonizing waiting period.

As the baby-by-science date drew ever nearer, our focus tended to shift towards the more utilitarian. We couldn't help but speculate how our lives would change ten short months from now. We started thinking about which room would go to the baby, where a crib would go, what color the room should be, and we even started making plans for remodeling the family room to make it more kid-friendly.

Kiersten was in full baby-name swing, thinking of what she would name a girl, a boy, and further—what she would name twin girls as well as twin boys. Her specialty, however, was girl names. The *nom du jour* was a family name of sorts (my side)—Celia. Celia Bea, to be specific. Better yet, it was a Swedish name and she thought it would go better with a fair-skinned, blonde-haired, blue-eyed baby than her other favorite name, Flora Mae.

"I tried to get Vince and Kara to use Flora because I think it would really suit one of their little Samoan darlings . . . " she said.

"And they were rude enough to not have a fourth kid for you?"

"Very funny."

Please tell me there isn't a Petunia Picklebottom bag called "Sold on Celia."

I spent my idle time thinking about college funds, whether I should get my rotator cuff repaired from years of baseball abuse in case we had a boy so I could toss either the "old rawhide" or the "old pigskin" around, and, of course, the inevitable panic about global warming and the general geo-political state of the world and the kind of place into which we were bringing a baby.

More pragmatically, we discussed godparents, daycare, schools, work schedules, circumcision, you name it. In sum, we had the red carpet dusted off and ready to roll.

We thought it might be fun to have twins.

– Sam Frustaci, *Time,* June 3, 1985,
regarding his wife's use of fertility pills
that led to septuplets

JUST A LITTLE PRICK

IVF was pretty simple in concept. The process itself wasn't that different from the "traditional method"—it merely made creating a baby more of a team sport and there was no sex involved, and consequently, no cuddling. Still took eggs, still took sperm, but you needed highly trained people at every step of the way to produce, extract, fertilize, and implant. Consider it the procreation Special Olympics.

Instead of nature's way, you got the pharmacy's way. Substitute ultrasounds for foreplay. In lieu of intercourse, she got a wand with eggs inserted into her uterus. Instead of post-coital endorphins, she got two days of bed rest. There were so many people taking turns putting objects up your wife's hoo-hoo, you wondered if you should start selling admission tickets.

Roughly a week before we were to begin, we met with Susan again to discuss the injections that Kiersten needed before and after the egg retrieval procedure. I had heard that I would be giving Kiersten some kind of injection, but I didn't necessarily realize that we were talking 12 weeks of daily injections and with 22 gauge needles (intermuscular injections take big needles). Incidentally, this could come in handy if you were really, really pissed off at your wife.

I was no fan of needles. At the age of 18, I visited the doctor regarding the thumb I had just smashed while playing basketball. He took an x-ray, left the room, and while he was gone a nurse came in to give me some kind of booster shot. It seemed innocent enough, but after she left, I recall feeling a little funny. The doctor returned with my x-ray, held it up to the window for examination and said, "You've got to come check this out." (Turned out it was a really impressive compound fracture.)

I eagerly hopped off the table, and with a thud, subsequently collapsed on the floor. My legs were worthless, jelly-like, and I had no shot at standing. Apparently, I had some kind of aversion to needles. Several times since then, I've had near fainting spells from blood being drawn or from simply seeing an IV drip. I swear I almost fainted once just from seeing the blood donation truck pull up on my campus in college. I also turned my head every time they broke out a needle while watching *Grey's Anatomy*.

We made our way into Susan's office. She produced what appeared to be a junkie's tool chest. There were needles, vials, bandages, and other such paraphernalia.

"So your first round of shots is to develop healthy eggs for extraction, okay? Just take the mixing needle…"

As she unsheathed the fencing sword that she called a needle, the hairs on my neck stood on end and Kiersten immediately started to silently cry. This was a terrifying needle—so large it seemed you could pump gas through it. Susan realized we were both moments from apoplectic shock and clarified, "Oh, now don't worry—this is just the mixing needle, you don't want to inject with this needle."

You were 15 seconds away from my lunch all over your lap, lady.

"So with this mixing needle, draw one cc of sodium chloride—hold the needle like so…" Susan held the vial of sodium chloride at a 45 degree angle, and drew out the fluid with one hand. It was an impressive display of coordination, but she probably hadn't ever had to masturbate, turn pages in a magazine, and aim into a cup before.

Amateur.

"Now you mix your sodium chloride with the Repronex, which is a follicle stimulating drug. Just insert the needle into the vial, and empty out the contents. Make sure the Repronex dissolves. Remove the needle and take out your Follistim pen…"

She pulled out what literally appeared to be a pen, pocket hook on the cap and all.

Oh, how fucking clever— let me just take this to work with me—nobody will notice!

The pen had a plunger which could be controlled by dialing up the number of cc's of medicine you needed. Very slick.

"Queue up 150 cc's of Follistim, insert it into the Repronex with the sodium chloride and mix, okay?"

"So, just how messed up will Kiersten get if I screw up the mixing process…she won't start growing a beard or something, will she?" I asked.

"No, but she might not grow any eggs either," Susan rebutted.

Touché.

Susan finished up giving us our mixing directions for the shots. It was all a total blur to me already, but fortunately someone had seen fit to type up the instructions for us to take home. I couldn't help but think it was because somebody's wife had grown a beard in the past, but I didn't feel like debating that with Susan right now, seeing as she had a veritable carving knife in her fist.

She picked up an item off of her desk. It had the look of a white coaster with a fleshy dome protruding from it, probably no more than about five inches in diameter.

"When you insert the needle, you want to do it perpendicular to the skin. Do it quickly but firmly enough to penetrate the muscle, okay?"

She proceeded to give this poor accessory a shot with her needle. It looked simple enough.

"Why don't you give it a try," instructed Susan as she handed me the needle and the unfortunate imitation buttocks.

I was not thrilled about even looking at this needle, but with my wife sitting at my side grimacing at the idea of daily injections, I needed to exude confidence.

I had to make this look easy.

I took the needle and held it like a dart as Susan instructed me to do, sizing up my target. With conviction, I pulled the needle back towards me and thrust it forward for the injection.

To everyone's horror, but understandably more so to Kiersten's, the needle which I had fearlessly attempted to inject into our friend, the fake bottom, bent at a right angle like a tricycle spoke under a sumo wrestler.

Kiersten covered her mouth with both hands, her eyes bulging in disbelief.

I started laughing out loud, mostly because I felt sorry for the imitation epidermis I had just disfigured. I immediately asked Susan for a new needle, which she supplied me, and I subsequently performed multiple near-perfect injections, but the damage had been done. I wouldn't initially be giving injections to my wife—she had already hatched the plan to come into the clinic after work and have the other nurse, Linda, perform the injections for us.

I, on the other hand, was relegated to practicing on an orange at home. And what a sad fate that orange met. As far as ways to die if you're a fruit, this had to be barely second to being featured on the infomercial for the Juice Master or perhaps just being smashed into a garbage disposal.

As Kiersten defected to Linda for the first week, I practiced diligently and became quite adept at injections (and the orange was so full of progesterone that it had C-cup breasts…). But my inaugural injection was to be preceded by harvesting the fruit of the Repronex and Follistim injections—namely, lots and lots of eggs.

It was time to do the "retrieval."

RETRIEVAL

Kiersten had felt progressively "bloated" throughout the week. This was explained by the two ultrasound appointments where Granderson scoped her insides to discover many growing "follicles," which I learned were the sacs of fluid that surrounded maturing eggs. Each follicle was measured by the doctor and recorded by Linda during the appointments.

"13 by 15," the Doc said. I believe he was measuring the length and width of each follicle in millimeters.

"Is that good?" I asked.

"Well, we like them to be of similar size; that way we know they'll mature at about the same time," he responded.

"Okay, so that's good then?" I asked yet again.

"Eight on the left side," the Doc said to Linda as she transcribed.

"Is that good?" I repeated.

"We're looking for quality here, not necessarily quantity," he replied, then continued, "11 by 11, 12 by 14, and…12 by 15… seven on the right side."

"Is that good?" I reiterated.

"Yes, everything is good," he said.

You could have said that the first time I asked you...

I couldn't help asking stupid questions. I was completely out of my element and it was the only tool in my toolbox. I felt as if I had been offered the chance to observe brain surgery, or a shuttle launch, or perhaps the destruction of a planet by a supernova: it was truly fascinating, but I had absolutely no context of what was up or down.

With healthy and copious eggs at the ready, a retrieval appointment was set to get those receptive little nuggets of goo out and ready for Ken's tender back-room union with my boys.

We arrived at the clinic early. Fortunately, we were the only appointment that morning—the entire office was dedicated to Kiersten's care. Linda took her back to a changing room to get in a medical gown and blanket, and then she was shuttled to a room where we both met the anesthesiologist.

The room was minimalist and just a tad creepy. There was a surgical table replete with stirrups, some kind of medical contraption with lots of pretty buttons, an ultrasound machine, and some cabinets with medical supplies. Additionally, I noticed one wall appeared to have a removable hunk of plywood with two handles on each side. There was nothing Easter-fun about this egg-retrieval room, and if it weren't for the thousands of dollars we'd already invested in this ridiculous process, I might have whisked poor Kiersten right out of there.

The anesthesiologist was already slipping my wife into a near-coma as Granderson arrived. He removed the mysterious piece of plywood from the wall, revealing a plexiglass sliding window which provided a view of Ken and his lab of egg and sperm mysteries.

"Your chili dog will be right up," the Doc cracked.

Now that's actually funny.

It was time for me to go. I was led out to the lobby where I waited for the next 45 minutes, reading all about how to improve my golf swing by placing whimsical obstacles all around me and avoiding them in my backswing and follow through. At that particular moment, I couldn't believe how insignificant and stupid this magazine was.

People get paid to pull this stuff out of the blue, I just know it. You could write, 'Improve your drive by wearing your wife's underwear' and there would be golf courses full of middle-aged men pulling thongs out of their cracks.

My suspense led to impatience which led to irritability which led to high stress. I had to know what was going on back there. What the hell could be taking so long?

The Doc emerged, his gait oozing confidence.

"Sixteen eggs," he said proudly.

"Sixteen!" I mimicked, not knowing what I was supposed to expect. "Is that good?"

"Yes, that's good."

You learn well, Doc.

I visited Kiersten as she was recovering. She was still quite groggy from the anesthesia and in a fair amount of discomfort following the procedure. They had warned us that she might need to "take it easy" for a couple of days, but she was feeling as if she could use a couple of days without moving an inch. There wasn't much I could do for her, so I sat and held her hand and tried to ask her questions that had nothing to do with infertility, eggs, children, or anything about this room we were in.

"Michael, 9:30—time to do your thing," said Ken, interrupting my attempt at distracting Kiersten. It was time to see if all that good beverage behavior paid dividends. I needed to get Ken some boys to match up with Kiersten's 16 girls.

With a sigh, I took the paper bag from Ken and endured the walk of shame down the hallway to the collection room.

I stepped in, performed my obsessive-compulsive locking ceremony on the door, took out the familiar instructions and oversized collection receptacle, and sat on the couch which hated its life.

"Hello, Geena—I'm back."

*   *   *

As an aside, my three months without recreational and/or heavy reckless drinking had an unexpected impact. About six weeks into my habit-crushing prescribed hiatus, I began to notice a bit of a change in my appearance. I was losing weight. I can't really tell you what I started out at, but I decided to buy a scale just for the hell of it. If I didn't like the number it gave me, I vowed to smash it into bitty little pieces. Conservatively, I had lost about eight to ten pounds. By the end of my three month sentence, I dropped somewhere between 15 and 20 pounds. This fact, coupled with the information Ken was about to deal me, made me want to join a religious cult and vanish for a while.

Ken performed an analysis after my recent round in the collection room. Apparently, he'd never seen such a dramatic turnaround. He shared the information with the rest of the clinic, and discovered that they too had never seen such a stark change in count and motility.

They bandied about the resulting data from my analysis with great joy and amazement. Imagine if your office water-cooler talk was all about sperm. What's more, imagine your mother-in-law telling you what wonderful sperm you have. What a perfectly insane reality I was living in.

So there I was, a piece of carry-on luggage lighter, with a miracle change in the performance of my boys. Everyone was so congratulatory. I was mortified. All it took was throwing the bottle away for three months and my entire body could change like this. What an unnerving, humbling experience. The clinic staffers seemed to start looking at me as if I had grown up at a distillery. Frankly, I couldn't stop thinking about where the nearest one might be to help me forget all of this.

FAMILY IN A BOTTLE

D r. Granderson employed a sort of sliding scale of natural reproduction. We weren't candidates for Clomid (a relatively non-invasive hormonal treatment to encourage follicle stimulation) or an IUI (intrauterine insemination, where they clean up the sperm and inject it into the uterus). He did, however, choose to attempt a quasi-natural fertilization by dumping my sperm onto some of Kiersten's eggs in lieu of choosing the sperm and injecting them into the egg themselves (ICSI— intracytoplasmic sperm injection).

I envisioned Ken holding up a little plastic cup of my boys and turning them upside down on a dish full of eager eggs, smacking the back of the cup like a near-empty bottle of mustard. "Get in there and do your job, fellas!" I could hear him say.

Apparently, it wasn't nearly that much fun. Ken parceled off half of the eggs and very clinically mixed in a cleaned-up sample of sperm.

The result? Bupkis. The two groups got along like Republicans at an LGBT conference. Nothing fertilized. We were suddenly left with eight healthy eggs instead of sixteen.

Ken got busy on the ICSI, searching out studly looking sperm, nabbing them like a rodeo cowboy, and forcefully injecting them into the eggs. I couldn't help but wonder if they were very confused about where all the cervical mucous went. Although our first eight were a total loss, we were pretty fortunate with this group and got 100 percent fertilization.

After a brief period of anxiety about how many to put back in (yes, that's back in Kiersten's uterus), the doctor recommended re-inserting three fertilized eggs during the transfer process (he referred to our three as "two and a half" since one of them really didn't look that great, and I found myself already protective of my potential offspring... I mean, who the hell were you calling a half-pint, anyway?!).

The remaining five went the way of Ted Williams, into a deep and hopefully peaceful cryogenic freeze. Would we need to use them in the future? Hopefully not, because that would mean this round failed. But if this round worked, what would we do with the frozen embryos? It was a moral issue we weren't prepared for by the clinic, and something we barely even considered when we started the process. Neither of us was comfortable with this particular territory but we didn't have too many options at this point, and it seemed relatively low on the list of immediate problems at the moment.

*   *   *

Based on a friend's advice, Kiersten had been undergoing routine acupuncture—apparently, there was some evidence that it aided in fertility. Funny, she didn't buy my argument that daily fellatio aided in fertility, but she'd sign up for more freaking needles. Regardless, she had arranged to have the acupuncturist treat her prior to the transfer this morning—ostensibly to "prime the pump." I'd seen way too many damned needles in the last few weeks, so I wanted no part of it and summarily ducked out.

The transfer process was surprisingly simple (although, to give Kiersten her due, I wasn't the one in stirrups). Back in the "chili dog" retrieval room, Ken handed the fertilized eggs to Granderson. The eggs were essentially "stuck" to the end of a long, very narrow catheter, which was used to safely drop them onto Kiersten's cervical lining. In approximately five minutes, the three fertilized eggs were resting in an ideal environment. Everyone, including the two of us, was extremely optimistic.

Kiersten needed to stay where she was for at least an hour, and afterwards she was to engage in as little activity as possible. As we sat there in the room, we were both tremendously excited, almost giddy with anticipation. But just to be clear to my would-be potential bundles of joy, I whispered to Kiersten's abdomen, "Hello in there… I'm sorry, but one of you has to go…"

*　　*　　*

Considering how long everything seemed to take during the IVF process, the time between the transfer and finding out if one or more eggs implanted was unexpectedly brief. Approximately two weeks after the transferring of the fertilized eggs, a blood test could be performed to identify a pregnancy.

Kiersten and I spent the majority of that time discussing what we'd do if, by chance, we got triplets. We figured we had to be prepared for the most difficult outcome, because nothing else had been easy to this point (after all, not all three eggs needed to implant in order to make triplets—one of the implanted eggs could divide and you had the possibility of an identical pair and a third being fraternal... weird, huh?). We also covered our bases on the issue of twins: whether we would do bunk beds in their room, how we would handle child care, and what we'd do if Kiersten wound up on bed rest early on due to any complications. We were off and running, burgeoning parents in the making.

As the week dragged on, Kiersten started noticing the early signs of pregnancy. A trace amount of cramping, pronounced blue veins across her chest, nausea, noticeable growth in her breasts (hip-hip...hooray!), etc., etc. She called the clinic to ask if all of this was possible, and they confirmed that in some women, signs of pregnancy do start very early.

In an effort to distract ourselves from the stress and anticipation associated with knowing a doctor has just inserted three fertilized embryos in your wife's uterus and you have to wait two weeks for the results, we popped in a movie and made some popcorn. Incidentally, this was typically the time I'd have a couple of beers and maybe a martini—but instead I mixed diet tonic water with lime to fool myself into thinking it was a gin and tonic. I sipped, smiled, and thought, "Nope, not fooling anyone..."

Kiersten had left the room as I was concocting my mind-game beverage and as I was struggling to enjoy it, she returned with a stark look on her face.

"You okay?" I asked.

"I'm bleeding. A lot."

"Is that at all normal?"

"I don't know," she said. "I'm calling Linda."

My crappy drink was rendered insignificant. We had other friends who didn't have difficulty conceiving children, but had real problems with frequent miscarriages. We had heard of stories of women who actually got their uterus sewn shut in order to prevent miscarriage after the first few months. I sat and wondered if it was possible that after having to go to such extremes to conceive, we would have to face the prospect of encountering trouble in keeping them.

After a brief conversation with Linda, it turned out some degree of bleeding was perfectly normal.

Phew.

I could get into the specific details of their conversation about the color, consistency, and a variety of other descriptors, but you might be reading this with a sandwich in your other hand. And I hate to ruin a good sandy.

Feeling as if we'd dodged a bullet, we settled in for a movie on the couch.

With crappy beverages.

*   *   *

After our little bleeding scare the night before, Kiersten decided to go against the advice of our clinic. Although she didn't tell me until later, she did exactly what the clinic told her not to do—she purchased and took a home pregnancy test two days before her appointment to have her blood drawn. I believe they told you not to do this because most women did not produce the pretty pink lines which indicated pregnancy, since it was so early, which threw them into a fit of depression, when in fact, they very well could have been pregnant but it would simply not show up on a test save for a blood sample.

Her test was the exception. Two pink lines.

She called a couple of friends to confirm that this, indeed, meant what she thought it meant ... and to share her excitement. She hatched a plan to have the blood test a day early to surprise me with the news of which she had premature knowledge.

She was pregnant.

COUNTING OUR CHICKENS

My phone rang at about 9:30 in the morning.

"Hi, this is Michael," I said in my standard work phone-answering tone, a mix between being happy to hear from you and sounding irritated that you just interrupted something important.

"It's negative," she said.

"What?"

"I took the blood test early—the clinic said I could go in today. I wanted to surprise you. It's negative."

"What...What?? Negative? So there's no chance at all?"

Not three.

Not two.

Not a thing.

I was dumfounded.

Negative wasn't even on my registry of possibilities.

"No...nothing took," she said, distant.

She was audibly crying.

"I'm coming home," I said.

I hung up the phone, but I was stuck staring into nothingness, expressionless.

I took note of this feeling. It was a sensation like a warm blanket of desperation pulled up my back and over my head. It disabled me, leaving me helpless and confused.

There was no one to ask 'why' because nobody knew why.

I couldn't cry because I didn't understand.

All I could think to do was look down and put one foot in front of the other.

I left work without notice.

Lights on, computer running, meetings unattended, unfinished business scattered across my desk...

Fuck.

*I could be content that we might procreate
like trees, without conjunction, or that
there were any way to perpetuate
the world without this trivial
and vulgar way of coition.*

– Sir Thomas Browne (1605-1682)

WHY NO BABY?

For years now, one of our favorite places to eat in town has been a Cantonese restaurant which we affectionately called "Sam's" because that was the name of the cook and co-owner. It had a more formal name, The New Peking Restaurant, but "Sam's" was much more efficient among friends. Sam's wife, Jessica, was the main waitress and hostess. They had a teenage daughter who occasionally worked at the restaurant, as well as a toddler who couldn't possibly be more adorable.

Sam's was housed in a ramshackle former single-family home on a busy street sandwiched in between a historic neighborhood featuring rows of early 1900s craftsman-style homes and less savory quick-lube shops, car washes, and motels that rented by the week. The exterior was in desperate need of repair. The cedar shingle roof likely carried a thirty-year guarantee about fifty years ago and the siding hadn't seen a fresh coat of paint in over a decade. The interior was eclectic, with traditional Chinese décor juxtaposed with giant Heineken cardboard cutouts. Hundreds of old fortune tickets were wedged between exposed bricks on the walls flanking the vinyl booths, a parting gift from patrons indulging in a form of fortune-cookie-graffiti entertainment in between tea and the main course.

But the look and feel of Sam's wasn't the draw; it was the food and their wonderful personalities that brought you back. While I didn't know the story of Sam and Jessica, I could almost guarantee their real names were not Sam and Jessica. They had likely immigrated here as adults, as evidenced by a still-present language barrier, but they definitely got by on the English they did know. Sam was roughly 5' 6" and sinewy—he appeared to have about three percent body fat—and he never stopped smiling. He was always having fun with his customers, complete with a biting sense of humor. Upon each visit, you could be assured of a personal visit from Sam to your table. Chances were, if you had been there a couple of times, he would even remember your name.

By now you've got to be wondering what the hell Sam's has to do with procreation. For Kiersten and me, Sam's became an ongoing painful joke of sorts—a microcosm of implicit and unknowing irreverence towards our situation. For years, Sam and Jessica would ask us the same questions, but what had always been in good fun became fairly painful as we began learning the challenges we faced in creating offspring.

"Michael, Michael, how are you?" Sam asked enthusiastically.

"I'm well, Sam, how are you?"

"Oh, good good!" he responded, eyes widening with excitement. "Kay-eer-Stun, you are looking so beautiful!" he said, butchering Kiersten's name—but by now, it was an endearing hack job.

"You have baby?" he asked.

"No, Sam—no baby."

"Ohhh...no baby? You like borrow my baby? Maybe you like and you have one?" he proposed.

We laughed, but of course, we had heard this sales pitch a dozen times by now.

Sam slid over towards Kiersten and gestured toward me. "Why he give you no baby? He seem like good, strong husband—should give you baby!"

"Oh, maybe someday, Sam," she said.

Just tell him my sperm are crap and see what he does.

"Okay then, enjoy your dinner. Thank you for coming."

Sam's barbs were all in good fun, but if his Mongolian Beef dish wasn't so good, I couldn't say we would keep coming back for the punishment. As we recovered with some tea, Jessica brought the traditional egg-flower soup for Kiersten and hot-and-sour soup for me.

"HI MIKE, HI KURSTIN."

Jessica was as pleasant as could be, but if I could bestow two new characteristics on her, it would be a voice that was several octaves lower than her current dead-waking shrill and that she would learn the definition of "inside voice." But we loved her nonetheless.

"YOU HAVE BABY???"

Kill me.

"No, no baby."

"NO BABY? WHY NO BABY???"

Kill me.

"Well, we've got a dog that keeps us pretty busy,"

"OKAY, ENJOY!!!"

How are you, do you have a baby, enjoy your meal. It was the same recipe each visit, whether we were dining in or taking out. As our struggle to procreate wore on, the "WHY NO BABY" mantra became a bit of comic relief every time we were reminded of our plight by chance or by people too ignorant or insensitive to know better. It helped us find humor in what wasn't funny at all.

In that way, Sam's was really a blessing for us.

BRUISED FRUIT

W*hy?*
       When it comes to infertility that is a particularly testy question.

Why me?

Why us?

Why *not* us?

Since I possessed an advanced degree in a social science, I turned to the research for answers in an effort to address the issue of 'Why me?'. Did I do this to myself? Did someone do this to me?

It turned out causes of male infertility varied widely, and it wasn't always easy to find a smoking gun. As far as the studies themselves went, findings typically led to "may cause" assertions and rarely to direct causality.

A quick scan of the Internet revealed great information from reputable medical institutions and research facilities, all the way down to wing-nut folks solving everything with magical salves (as tends to happen with Internet searches, I suppose). By most accounts, there are nearly eight million infertile individuals in the United States— and 40% of the infertility is caused by the man. Roughly half of that 40% will never father children due to irreversible damage.

There was a laundry list of no-brainers when it came to what's bad for your boys. Reading the way that our medical professionals described them provided some decent comedy:

"Testicular Overheating" —get out of the hot tub and stop wearing your too-tight striped jockeys from the 1980s.

"Substance Abuse" —yes, if you repeatedly did lines of coke and made out with your bong more than your partner, you were going to have very confused sperm. You were also likely to be a complete miscreant, but as they'd say in the world of research, "that requires additional study." On the subject of substance abuse, the University of Maryland Medical Center website put it so diplomatically: "Sperm actually have receptors for certain compounds in marijuana that may impair the sperm's ability to swim." No shit? They left out the part where the sperm decides to stop swimming and hitches a ride with their asshole roommate to go to Krispy Kreme and chortle at the funny hats the staff wear while scarfing a dozen doughnuts.

"Testicular Trauma" —you got kicked in the junk.

"Malnutrition and Nutrient Deficiencies" —you thought the food pyramid actually represented a giant slice of pizza with everything on it.

"Obesity" —now, this was cited on several resource guides and each one of them said that research was not definitive. So why make a big man question himself? Could it be that obese men couldn't make babies because

nobody wanted that hefty dude gyrating on top of them? In all seriousness, there have been studies that link obesity and decreased sperm production—and given the direction of our waist-lines in the Mc-U.S., I think we'll see more about this in the future.

"Vasectomy" —file this under "duh."

"Anabolic Steroids" —file this under "ironic."

Perhaps the more likely explanation for growing male infertility rates was our changing environment. According to a Reproductive Genetics Center study, .05 percent of men were functionally sterile (sperm counts below 20 million) in 1938. Today that rate is eight to 12 percent. Some studies argued the rate of male infertility was growing at a rate of one to two percent each year. Many researchers pointed to environmental factors, but the causal link was extremely difficult to demonstrate. We wound up with a battery of chemical, pharmaceutical, and environmental possibilities for male infertility. Heavy metals, hydrocarbons, varnishes, glues, solvents, pesticides, oxidants (free radicals), etc.—all exhibited effects on male fertility, but determining statistically significant causality was another matter. However, it was probably safe to say that if you worked in a rubber factory or if you finished floors for a living and you were just getting to the family planning part of life, you should move to a state where IVF was covered by your HMO.

I thought back over the course of my life, struggling to pinpoint what it was that I had done that could have impacted the ability of my boys to swim straight, swim strong, and do what nature intended for them to do—fertilize an egg.

I could recall no testicular issues save for the rocket ground ball that I couldn't glove.

We didn't have a hot tub. Hell, I didn't even regularly ride a bike.

My diet was okay.

I was fairly certain I hadn't had a vasectomy.

No steroids. My biceps proved it.

No obesity, though I could trim 10 to15 lbs.

That left substance abuse, environmental issues, and "unknown."

I had definitely exposed myself to a bevy of harsh chemicals over the last two years as I restored a century-plus old home. Stripping paint with a heat gun, wood stains, polyurethanes, wood conditioners, drywall, sanding God-knows-what off of floors and siding, and thousands of square feet of latex paint. But could a brief exposure like this have such a devastating effect? Probably not.

Yes, I've dabbled in "substances." For a moment, I panicked as I recalled months where I was more accustomed to the cloud of marijuana smoke in my house than I was to the oppressiveness of daylight sun. I once had hair down to the middle of my back. I grew a massive beard. I was a quasi-hippie gen-X'er who was pissed off that the American dream of my parent's generation was long gone—and the best way to fix it was to buy a bong taller than you and pay daily homage to it.

But my folks were right: It was a phase. A fun one for sure, but just a phase.

That moment of anxiety was cut short by what I had observed around me for the last six months. Everywhere I turned, people who had more than 'dabbled' in drugs, including many who still made it a daily habit, had successfully produced offspring. Most of my friends had a much longer rap sheet than I when it came to their youthful indiscretions, and they were surrounded by biological bambinos.

So again, I have to ask, why me?

The right to procreate is not guaranteed,
explicitly or implicitly, by the Constitution.

– Robert Bork

BAD NEWS BEARING

It had occurred to us that we might not get pregnant after the first round of IVF. But after two weeks of touching every possible base on the highway of signs of early pregnancy, we were both at a loss as to what to do now that we knew we weren't.

When Kiersten spilled the beans about breaking the rules and taking an early pregnancy test two days before her blood test, it hit me that the bleeding she had the day before probably represented a miscarriage, a fact that Kiersten obviously already knew. The good news was we *had been* pregnant. We knew we could get to that point, which was a sizable hurdle in the procreation Special Olympics. But it didn't really help us swallow this bitter fucking pill.

Roughly 48 hours had passed since our "negative." We had pretty much holed ourselves up and ordered delivery for our daily squares in order to avoid the outside world. But enough time had passed that everyone to whom we had previously disclosed our timeline was growing impatient. To their credit, they were curious and nervous. The phone started to ring.

And ring.

And ring some more.

God bless them for caring, but regurgitating bad news was like being forced to watch reruns of the Chevy Chase show—wasn't good the first time and grew even more painful each time thereafter. I had several conversations that ran about the same:

"Hi, Michael?!" an irritatingly upbeat voice would inquire.

"Yes."

"Is Kiersten there?"

I'm fine, how are YOU?!

"Yeah, but uh…she's not feeling too hot."

"Can I talk to her?" the voice persisted.

"Well, I don't think she's in the mood to talk right now."

"I'm just so concerned, I haven't heard from her in two days, could you put her on the phone?" the voice instructed.

"Well, it didn't work and I think she'd rather not talk right now."

"What didn't work?" the irritatingly naïve voice asked.

"The test was negative."

"I don't understand," the voice proclaimed.

If you need a picture, a world-class circle is available at Granderson's…

"Well, neither do we, but the test came back negative."

"Is Kiersten okay?"

Oh, yes—she's thumbing through Pottery Barn Kids, giggling with glee…

"Um… well… I guess she's…uh…doing about as well…as you would…expect," I stammered.

"What are you going to do?" the voice that I'd have liked to beat senseless asked.

Steal your kid and move to Senegal.

"I don't know. I'd better get back to Kiersten. Thanks for calling."

I felt badly for those who decided to wait to call because their conversations were decidedly different:

"Hi, Michael!?" said the irritatingly upbeat voice.

"Negative...No, we're not sure what we're going to do ... thank you for calling."

There should have been a manual available for new infertility patients that strongly advises against telling friends and acquaintances what you're undertaking unless you were remarkably strong-willed individuals who loved to deliver your own painfully bad news, and deliver it many times. In addition to finding ourselves in the uncomfortable position of backpedaling with our carefully-thought-out and well-intentioned baby plans, we also had to somehow politely tell our closest friends to stop asking about it. Kiersten, ever the student of propriety, forcibly willed her digits to dial the numbers of loved ones and friends who hadn't yet heard from us because it was just too rude to leave them hanging.

"Fuck them. They'll live. Can't they assume it didn't work if we don't call?" I had the answer for everything and it usually started with an expletive when I was feeling particularly cynical.

"We need to tell people," she said.

You are 1,000 times the person I am.

"Do what you have to, but remember this isn't about them, it's about you— and you need time to..."

"I need to tell everyone before I can deal with this. I just have to," she said.

She was right. This was how she ticked. The headline needed to be circulated. And so she called. Through it all, she was very gracious, positive, and upbeat. "Well, we know we can get pregnant, so that's the positive," she said. "We learned that we need to do ICSI for all of them from now on, so that's a good thing," she'd comment. "At least we have four fertilized eggs frozen that we can use in the future," she positively spun.

And when it was over, the phone was put away.

The light was turned off.

Shades drawn.

She slowly curled into a ball in the deepest corner of the couch.

She put her hands over her face.

And she quietly cried.

They are babies in waiting, life on ice.

– Claudia Wallis
Time, July 2, 1984,
on sperm cells frozen for preservation

THE REMATCH

"How many are frozen?" I asked.

I got the look that resembled the one wives gave their husbands when they forgot a wedding anniversary—apparently, this was a detail I should have tucked away in the very small 'important information' place in my brain.

"Four," Kiersten graciously reported.

"So that might give us two more shots, right?"

"Right," she confirmed.

With four fertilized embryos, the idea was that we could use two this time, and still have two left in case that round didn't work. We were both still a bit shell-shocked from the negative on the first go-round, but decided to jump right back in. Per Doc's instructions, we had to bide our time for about a month and a half while Kiersten waited for her period, went back on the birth control pill and then started her medication again. A word to the wise husband—Aunt Flo after hormone injections is a truly unwelcome guest. Because the hormones were designed to produce award-winning cervical lining—the equivalent of Four Seasons hospitality for the incoming embryo—the period could be far worse than usual, complete with crippling cramps and emotional fluctuations. It was also particularly enjoyable after a negative result, as I'm sure you can imagine.

This round would be easier, however. We weren't growing eggs, we didn't even have to worry about fertilization, motility, morphology, or any of that mess—and better yet, I didn't have to visit the collection room yet again. We just needed to get Kiersten's cervical lining into shape in order to create an appropriate welcome mat for some potential little ones.

Diligently, we started the shots. There was a general positive atmosphere surrounding this round, I believe simply due to the sheer power of statistics. You see, the first round had a roughly 40 percent chance. This frozen round stood about a 35 percent chance. Cumulatively, it was pretty unlikely that we wouldn't get pregnant with this round. After all, we were in our early thirties and in the most likely range of IVF success. Furthermore, we would have yet another pair of kids on ice just in case this one went awry. The future looked bright.

Unfortunately, neither of us were embryologists. If we were, we would have known that not all of the fertilized embryos were expected to survive the trip from cryogenic freeze to room temperature. If we lost one, that would surely cut our backup round short. And as expected, only three embryos wound up surviving the thaw.

Seeing our evident disappointment, Granderson tried to assure us that this wasn't something to fret about.

"Trying to choose which embryos are the best is really impossible," he posited. "We can identify the ones we think are the most likely to create a pregnancy, but really, it's a lot like moving shells around—we know there's a pregnancy in one of these embryos, we're just not sure which one. Sometimes, it's the ugliest embryo we have that produces the healthiest pregnancy. So what we have left from your first round could include one of those very healthy pregnancies. I'm fairly certain that this should work for you."

We confidently plowed forward with the hormone regimen, Kiersten's cervical lining looked fantastic in the ultrasounds, and before we knew it, the day of the transfer was upon us. Again, we found ourselves in the "chili dog" room with Granderson doing mysterious things with my wife's holiest of holies. The procedure took no more than 15 minutes, and Linda the nurse boasted that it was one of the smoothest transfers she had ever seen.

As instructed, we needed to wait for an hour before Kiersten was able to move around too much. As we waited, I speculated on an interesting fringe benefit of our current situation:

"You know what's great about using the frozen ones?"

"No, what?"

"If our kid winds up complaining about being cold when we can't afford to heat the house, we can tell them, 'Of course you're cold—you used to be completely frozen! Now quit complaining and put on your parka.' I mean, how many parents can say THAT?!"

*   *   *

Shortly after the transfer, Kiersten developed a bit of a fever and some flu-like symptoms. She called the clinic and they said to start taking a couple of Tylenol to control the fever. It was important to keep it "low grade" — which apparently covers anything below 100.

Despite her best efforts, the flu worsened. Soon, she was vomiting. It couldn't have been an ideal environment for an embryo implanting. We proceeded with the progesterone shots with as much faith as we could muster, but we both had a bad feeling due to the circumstances. Still, we thought of our friends who were in the first few weeks of pregnancy and actually rolled their car without any ill effects. We thought of friends who had pounded the pavement training for marathons, unwittingly putting at risk the pregnancy that they didn't yet know about, who had healthy babies. Examples of unknowing mothers engaging in risky behavior during the early stages of pregnancy abounded. Why not us? Why not our kid?

Two weeks passed painfully slow, like a fourth grader counting the days to the end of the school year. Regardless, I couldn't help wonder if we'd succeeded.

What would we name a boy?

I wonder what color we should paint the room?

How much should I put away for a college fund every month?

I should probably think about a gift for Kiersten when she delivers the baby.

Despite our previous experience, I was optimistic. This just had to work.

The office phone rang on a Thursday morning.

"Hi, this is Michael." I said in my most professional inquisitive tone.

"It's me."

That's not a good tone.

"I took the test early," she said.

Please don't tell me it's negative.

"It's negative."

…silence…

What was the appropriate response? They didn't make Hallmarks for this occasion.

…more silence…

Roughly 30 incredibly fucking uncomfortable seconds passed.

"I'm sorry," I said.

Kiersten was quietly crying.

Pause.

"You don't need to say anything. Just hang up the phone. I'll see you at home and we'll talk," I said. It was perhaps the best possible thing I could have suggested. After all, what was there to discuss when you were overcome with emotion due to particularly depressing news? The weather?

Her cell phone cut out.

I sat at my desk with the phone stuck to my ear, staring at some ridiculously insignificant graph I had been assiduously working on minutes ago.

A busy signal ensued.

I was frozen, staring at the computer screen.

Minutes passed, the screen saver kicked on and I watched the colorful Microsoft logo dance around my flat-panel monitor.

I slammed the phone down.

"Fuck."

For good measure, I slammed it again.

FOOT IN MOUTH DISEASE

I might not be described as a news hog, but I also didn't live in a cave. I'd seen the Earth's population trends: We were growing. It took babies to grow, I got it. I obviously recognized there were a lot of little tykes out there, but when we discovered that having a biological kid would take a medical miracle, the sheer number of rugrats and frequency of pregnancy announcements grew exponentially.

Everyone in sight had a baby or had one on the way. I swear to you my hometown was single-handedly keeping Huggies in business. What's more, these fortunate folks were so wholly consumed with kids that they spouted stories about them with the kind of recklessness that suggested they didn't know there might be someone within earshot who couldn't just crank kids out as if they were Catholics on a mission from God.

I couldn't fault overzealous parents because they were very excited and very proud. But I sure as hell didn't have to like them. By way of example, let's say someone was carrying on a conversation with a person with one leg; do you think they'd boast about the marathon they just ran? If you were chatting with an acquaintance who happened to be accompanied by their seeing-eye guide dog, would you ask, "Hey, did you see that game last night?"

That was how it felt every time someone announced their pregnancy or asked you when you were going to have kids when you couldn't have one of your own *au natural*. It was a verbal kick in the groin. And unless you were strong enough to divulge to the world that you were going through assisted reproductive treatment (they call this "ART" in the biz, but I find that acronym stupid and irritating, so I refuse to use it) then you had to sit there and take the beating like a happy little soldier.

For instance, take my wife's book club. You may know how these things tend to go: a dozen women spent a month reading a book (and I believe it is the rule of the universe that nine out of twelve annual books must be hand-selected by Oprah Herself); they all gathered at one of their respective homes to discuss the book, and out of this came good for all mankind. Okay, I added the last part—but I swear it was implied.

If you have friends in book clubs, you also know this was not how they worked. For many years, Kiersten's book club was a forum for gossip, scandal, and rumor accompanied by copious consumption of $10-and-under bottles of wine. It was a social hour drama society masked by the illusion of literature. My informal survey of participants suggested that on any given book club date, approximately 15 to 20 percent of the attendees actually read the book cover to cover. Talk about your husbands, chit-chat about your boyfriends, share saucy details about your flings, speculate who on your staff has had a boob job, but don't feel obligated to actually talk about the book (do bring the book, though, because most people don't have a dozen coasters).

As her book club attendees aged in recent years, scandal and rumor began to give way to birth announcements and discussions of poopy diapers and "can you believe what my kid did" drivel. On the most recent occasions, Kiersten would come home in a bit of a huff, pour a glass of wine, sit across from me and vent about the contents of the last three hours of conversation at her book club.

"So guess who's pregnant?"

"You? It's a MIRACLE!!!" I said, casting my hands in the air like I was signaling a field goal.

...glare...

"I have no idea, please... do tell..."

"Meredith. Can you believe that? They have a 16-month-old at home."

"Is that question rhetorical, or am I supposed to respond about whether or not I believe that?"

I wasn't the best at book club post-mortem.

A little tipsy from the wine, Kiersten fumed, "I'm just *so pissed*. Every time I go, someone announces she's pregnant and then that's *all* we talk about! We never talk about the book, we never talk about anything else about anyone's lives except for *pregnancy* and *babies*!"

From this day on, her book club was referred to as "Fertility Club" and although I tried to enlist the principles of *Fight Club* ("First rule of Fight Club is, you do not talk about Fight Club. The second rule of Fight Club is...you *do not* talk about Fight Club..."), each passing Fertility Club meeting was met with a greater sense of disquiet, anger, and disappointment.

Now, I wasn't shy about my feelings on this subject—I hated this stupid Fertility Club. Though I wasn't surprised this kind of conversation went on, what these women did to her demonstrated out-and-out ignorance. You could give them the benefit of the doubt and think that they couldn't have known Kiersten was going through this, but these were all very well educated women who were not oblivious to the fact that people everywhere struggled to have kids. I guarantee you each one of them knew someone who wrestled with failed attempts to become pregnant. With the exception of a few of them, this group made my wife feel like a failure as a woman on a monthly basis, and that was just flat rude.

Why did she keep going, you ask? This group was chock-full of Kiersten's longtime teaching pals and she'd be damned if she was going to get run out of a spinning circle. The girl was too damned stubborn to allow infertility to get in the way of something that was supposed to be fun and enriching—and I think each week, she hoped that the conversation would change for the better. How many kids could these chicks have, anyway?

But with every subsequent meeting, there was a new announcement. Each Fertility Club was filled with baby formula, diapers, daycare, exersaucers, high-chairs, car seats, rashes, and teething remedies; debates about circumcision and immunizations; and conversation about oh-my-boobs-are-so-sore-now. As the months passed, she loathed going and finding out who was newly pregnant.

She despised the smiles of anticipation directed at her, seeming to suggest, "You're next... join our club!"

"Well, nobody ever accused your friends of being sensitive to other people," I said. "Maybe when someone makes a pregnancy announcement, you should make some ridiculous announcement to make a point... maybe they'll get it."

And damn if she didn't.

All the ladies arrived, cheap bottles of wine in tow, and for many of them, baby carriers with drooling bundles inside. Once settled, Sarah smiled confidently, sat up straight and proclaimed, "Okay, everyone, I have an announcement to make..." Gasps of anticipation and whispers of "Oh, my gosh!" abounded, accompanied by that fake I'm-putting-my-hand-over-my-mouth-like-I'm-shocked thing that I'm convinced just about everyone can't stand.

"I'm pregnant."

Group hug.

Just as everyone's excitement settled down to a moderate boil and they began refilling their wine glasses, Kiersten spoke.

"Well, everyone, I have an announcement to make too."

Immediately, people looked at her belly.

They looked at her glass, full of wine.

They looked at her.

They looked back at her wineglass.

They did the hand-over-the-mouth thing that everyone can't stand.

"Well, upon the advice of Oprah, I decided to get sized and I'm proud to announce that I'm now a 'C' cup!"

Kiersten smiled with brassy confidence.

The group paused, and subsequently erupted with laughter.

I'm not sure if she got her point across, but she had fun at Fertility Club for the first time in recent memory. I'm pretty sure Sarah didn't appreciate Kiersten absconding with her thunder, but you know what?

Screw Sarah.

*   *   *

Another example for your consideration is my workplace. I worked in an ultra-politically-correct world with diversity training, workshops on sensitivity to co-workers complete with icebreakers and role playing, and conversations about having genderless bathrooms for the transgendered, among many other examples. I understood and respected these things. We even had to take special precautions over things like sponsoring a family during the holidays to make sure it didn't look like we were favoring a particular religion. If you were going to clothe the disadvantaged Catholics, you needed to find some under-privileged Lutherans, too.

However, when it came to babies, sensitivity was shown the door. Everyone... *everyone*...assumed that not only did everybody love babies, but that all of us could have babies, and certainly everyone liked to talk about who was having them. I'm sure I would never have noticed if I could have impregnated my wife with a snap of my fingers, but nevertheless, it was a remarkable thing to watch. What's more, with roughly one in five of the baby-making population having some form of fertility disability, there were many of us out there quietly taking routine workplace gut-shots.

I had heard rumors of one co-worker being pregnant and truthfully, I was very happy for her. But one Monday morning caught me completely off guard. There were *three* pregnancy announcements. Now, if I worked for a huge business, this would be one thing, but there were roughly 25 people who worked in the office, and most of them either had grown children or were not of child-bearing age anymore. Three represented about 40 percent of the likely child-rearing candidates in our office—and the staff went simply ape-shit gaga when the news came out.

First, due dates needed to be established and each staff member would relate which of their relatives had birthdays on or near that date, as if it was somehow a blessing to go ahead and have the kid. Then it was off to the races guessing the gender. Soon following was the name game. It was easy enough for me to simply shut my door and ignore them—bury myself in my work, put my headphones on and listen to something from my college radio days to take me back to a simpler time.

But now that my peers were procreating, the rest of the office wanted to know when I'd be "announcing." A colleague knocked at my door.

"Yeah."

"So did you hear who's pregnant?" she said.

"How could I not hear?" I responded, painted smile gracing my face.

"So it's your turn, you know," she posited.

Thanks for the fucking update.

"You don't say," I responded, trying to be as pleasant as possible given the circumstances.

"We're all waiting for you guys to announce, you know. Come on, Barr—get on the stick," she challenged.

Do you think this mouse cord could hold you if I tried to hang you with it?

Before I said something incredibly rude, I grabbed my gear and pretended I had a meeting to get to. "Thanks, I appreciate you all taking such an interest in our sex lives, but I've got to get to a meeting," I said as I brushed past her.

Despite my haste, I was caught by my boss on the way out.

"We probably need to meet today to talk about how this is going to affect our office," she instructed.

You mean how the staff is taking a pool to guess genders instead of actually working right now?

"I suppose we should," I deadpanned.

Unless I throw myself under a bus before our meeting.

"Wait, you're not expecting a kid, are you?" she asked.

Oh, I'm sorry—did you notice that I'm down? Please, kick away...

"No. Are you?" I asked—a risky question to pose to a woman nearing fifty. But it seemed fair, all things considered. She didn't answer. Suggesting a few possible times for our meeting, she shuffled off and I was left standing there, preparing for a meeting that would never take place.

I decided I deserved a coffee. A real coffee.

Returning with a double espresso in hand, I plopped down in front of my computer to resume my duties, believing that I could make it through the day if I just tried to keep busy. That's when an office-wide e-mail caught my attention. I'll spare you the actual text and just say that the office was throwing a baby shower and wanted us all to contribute money for a truck-load of gifts.

It then occurred to me that I should put a mug outside my door requesting donations for another round of IVF. I wondered how much income that would have generated. "Alms to the masturbating and impoverished," it could read.

A couple weeks of relative quiet helped me forget that day from hell. That was, until one of the expecting fathers started working his way through the staff, cubicle by cubicle, office by office, telling each and every one of us that they had found out what gender their baby was and what they were going to name it. Forget the fact that it was a colossal waste of time—it also seemed presumptuous to assume that any of us really gave a shit.

I could hear him drawing closer… he was two doors down.

"Hey, I just wanted to let you know that we're having a girl," he said.

Hey, I'm just wondering what the fuck you do around here?

"Yeah, we're naming her…" The name was inaudible, but frankly, they could have named her Hamburger Helper and I probably would have felt the same way.

I heard my co-workers feign excitement. It was amazing the number of times two people could use the word "awesome" during a conversation:

"We're having a girl"

"Oh, that's so awesome!"

"I got to see the ultrasound, it was so awesome."

"That's awesome for you, really—that's awesome."

"It's just so exciting, you know? I can't believe we're going to have a kid. It's just so awesome."

"That's so awesome for you guys…"

I was fortunate I worked on the ground floor. Despite that fact, I still eyed my windows to see if I could use them for an escape since they were useless for suicide.

Too late.

Knock, knock.

"What's up?" I asked, my face contorted in the "Thank you sir, may I have another?" grimace.

"I just wanted to let you know that we found out we're having a girl," he said.

I just wanted to let you know that I know you look at porn at work.

"Oh. Yeah, I heard… wow. That's um. Well, that's… awesome."

"Thanks. Aren't kids just great?"

Oh, right— all those kids that you know I don't have…

"Oh, yes—great. Really great. Great, great. Super great. Congratulations."

I picked up my phone and responded as if it just rang.

"Hi, this is Michael…"

He moved to the next office. I wasn't sure if he bought it, but I really didn't care.

What made this worse was that he was a guy I cared about. I really did wish the best for him, but I was just so sick and tired of the baby talk, I couldn't muster any enthusiasm for him. I was constantly reminded of the fact that I couldn't produce a child of my own. I was repeatedly taunted by unwitting co-workers in this place that was supposed to be so ultra-sensitive to others. Every day, I went to work dreading the charade I had to maintain to get myself through the painful inquiries about my life and the side-conversations about babies, cribs, rockers, baby joggers, you name it.

And I didn't know how much more of this I could take.

BODY BY SAM

With round two in the books and nothing but swings-and-misses, we turned to comfort food. This was reason 3,344 to get take-out—inability to procreate. Reason 3,345 was if you received an overdraft notice in the mail from your bank. And that was often—especially when you were doing in-vitro. But again, I digress.

We decided that we needed the soothing and healing power of New Peking. Sam's Mongolian Beef was just calling to us and I couldn't wait for a cup of hot-and-sour soup—which, by the way, was Sam's secret weapon against all sickness. He claimed he had a cup of it every day and it kept him healthy in perpetuity. Nobody would argue with him, either—this soup was so spicy that you felt like you should hold your eyeballs in place while you ate. We knew there was a possibility of some baby talk, but it was all in good fun and we figured our skin was thick enough…and frankly, the food was good enough to take it.

After a quick rock-paper-scissors competition, Kiersten found herself driving to New Peking. Walking in, she was greeted with the typical enthusiasm.

"AH, KURSTEN! SO LONG TIME! YOU HAVE BABY?!"

Jessica wasted little time in tossing the first dagger.

"No, no baby. I'm just here to pick up an order."

As she dealt with the register, Jessica leaned back and yelled to the kitchen in what was likely Mandarin. Given the fact that neither of us spoke Mandarin, we were really never quite sure what language they used between the two of them. They could have had their own code for all we know. But whatever she said not only woke any dead folks in a four-block radius, it also brought Sam out from the back.

"Oh, Ka-Eer-Stun, how are you?" asked Sam.

"I'm good, thanks, Sam. How are you?"

"Oh, good, good. So…you leave Mike at home?"

"It's just my turn to pick up, I guess,"

"Ah, I see—you good wife!! You have baby yet?"

"No, no babies."

Sam packed traditional to-go Chinese boxes in a paper bag.

"No baby? Why no baby? You should have baby!"

"Yeah, well—I guess it's just not that simple for us."

"You like to borrow my baby? Maybe you like baby, have one of your own!"

Sam was putting the finishing touches on our order, adding the rice and chopsticks into the bag when Kiersten cracked.

"You know, Sam, it's not an issue of whether or not we want to have a baby, it's just that it's not possible, okay?"

He froze.

Counting the change out, Jessica paused.

Sam looked at Jessica.
Jessica looked at Sam.
They both looked at Kiersten.
Sam broke the silence.
"More soy sauce?"

I have a high state of resentment for the conformity in this country. If you're not married and having children, it's like your life is empty or you're a communist meanie.

– Bill Maher

ROUNDING THIRD

This particular October Saturday morning was one of those Northwest days that made us amazed the rest of the world didn't want to live here. The sky was resplendent yet so wholly peaceful you'd swear Bob Ross just put oil to canvas in an inspired moment. The temperature was just shy of 50—perfect fall weather for two Scandinavians like us. This was reason 2,047 to eat breakfast out—great weather. Reason 2,048 was if the dog yawned and broke wind simultaneously, which was unfortunately quite frequently.

We armed ourselves with our most familiar threads— Kiersten in jeans and an argyle sweater with an elegantly distressed white button-down underneath, and me in over-sized jeans which had been used for a painting project once too often, a vintage button-down (with snap buttons, of course), and my corduroy jacket with the faux-sheepskin lining purchased in about 1990. Our destination was a favorite breakfast spot, Harris Avenue, where Kiersten no longer even needed to speak to order. One grunt for coffee, two for pancakes.

This was as happy as we had been in a while...and we were genuinely content. Rounds one and two were a distant memory—time had worn the pain down to an occasional ache. But we still clung to the hope that a biological brat was in our near future. As usual, an unhealthy dose of morning coffee, protein, and carbs produced more down-to-earth conversation.

"Do you think it will ever work?" asked Kiersten, making time in between slices of bacon.

"Will what work?"

"The in-vitro. Another round. Do you think it's ever going to work?"

"It has to."

"Why?"

I paused. No doubt, she could see the logic coming.

"Look at the statistics. I mean, every time you have roughly a 40 to 50 percent shot. If you do it enough, you're going to get the right result. If you flip a coin three times, chances are it'll come up heads once, right? There really aren't any major variables working against us. I've got enough healthy boys to ICSI in there, you're a young woman with plenty of eggs—the odds are on our side. I believe Granderson when he says it's a question of when, not a question of if."

"I guess you're more rational about it than I am. I'm just really worried about another negative," she said.

"Well, I'm worried about you and another negative too. Maybe I should order some padding for the walls in the guest room and we can just put you in there for a few days afterwards."

"Nice. Really sensitive." She folded her arms and leaned away from her food as if she were disinterested.

"I'm sorry… you know I'm just screwing with you."

The feast resumed…

"It's just so consuming, you know? Every part of your life is affected by something you have no control over…"

She took a bite and stared beyond me stoically, pontificating into the chaos of a dozen unrelated conversations. She sipped her coffee.

"And you've got to endure weeks of injections and inhalers and patches. The whole thing is so orchestrated and unnatural, it almost feels like you're cheating nature—that maybe we're just not supposed to have a kid. And then everyone else around you seems to remind you of the one thing you can't have… everyone else is either pregnant or having a baby."

The couple to my right glanced at us briefly, probably trying to figure out if we were fighting or just having a passionate conversation. I smiled at them. It was an expression somewhere between "thanks for your concern" and "mind your own fucking business." I was the master of this look by now.

"I know, babe. It's pretty horrific to go through everything we've been through and then come up empty."

The scars weren't just emotional, either. Kiersten's lower back had only recently started to look normal. Silver-dollar-sized bruises from the progesterone injections—black, brown, yellow, and purple—reminded both of us of our most recent failed attempt to conjure up a child with modern magic. Every time she reached into a cabinet above her head or picked anything up off of the floor was a reminder. They looked like battle scars. It hurt me to know I had put them there. It hurt worse to know it had ultimately been meaningless pain.

Regardless, we had decided to go for a third round of in-vitro. Ken and Granderson maintained that they had learned a good deal of information from the first two rounds and they, along with input from Mrs. G. (the embryologist and wife to Granderson), decided to change Kiersten's drug regimen in an attempt to produce a better quality egg. Free range, I hypothesized. Additionally, they were going to use a more aggressive in-vitro method called a "blastocyst"—often called a "blast," which I admit sounded pretty ridiculous… but hey, whatever works.

Now, IVF was pretty damned amazing to begin with, but I have to admit that the idea itself and the technology involved weren't beyond my realm of imagination. All in all, it was a logical enough process—our stuff didn't seem to really work well together, so we just gave it a boost through IVF. But this "blast" was a page out of science fiction for me.

A blastocyst stage embryo transfer took much of the guesswork out of the embryo selection process. It had all the ingredients of an ICSI transfer, except they now cultured and grew the embryos in the laboratory, watching to see which fertilized embryos continued to divide until forming a central cavity called the "blastocoel." It was at this stage that the embryos had a greater chance of survival since they were much more mature. Because they were so likely to produce a pregnancy, on the fifth or sixth day, just one or two were reinserted into the uterus instead of three or four. As the good doctor would say, "We don't want a basketball team." (Incidentally, every time I thought of the blast transfer, I pictured Dana Scully from *The X-Files* in her lab gown, crimson hair neatly tucked in a bun, leaning carefully over a micro-scope with a horrified expression gracing her pouty, freshly painted lips. She leans back and says, "Mulder, you're not going to believe this." I have the rest of that episode written in my head, but I guess that'll have to wait for another day.)

To our surprise, we were both extremely optimistic that this round would work. It simply felt as though the first two rounds allowed us to weed out some of the obstacles until the staff arrived at a process they were assured would produce a pregnancy. Furthermore, thinking back to our first round where Kiersten had produced sixteen healthy eggs and we achieved 100 percent fertilization with the ICSI bunch, even if this third round was not successful, we figured we would have at least two full rounds of frozen fertilized embryos to draw upon for future rounds. The odds were on our side.

We called and got on the books for February. Why the long delay? Recall from an earlier chapter that my wife was a planning freak, and therefore needed to ensure that the baby arrived at an appropriate time for her schedule. January was earlier than she preferred, but it allowed for two rounds thereafter to be at an acceptable time. As always, I nodded and went along—to do otherwise was futile.

For the next couple of months, we lived it up. We thoroughly enjoyed our lives without children while we could, as we were convinced one would join us in the New Year. While I didn't return to my old drinking ways, I flirted with them often ... even had a saucy affair with them a couple of times, which culminated in a trip to a resort-brewery with a dozen or so close friends. It was to be our last hurrah before we started building a family. When the New Year finally came, I gave a hearty middle finger to 2005 and gladly greeted 2006.

February arrived and we welcomed it with 22-gauge needles, bandages, cotton balls, small vials of saline solution, and of course, Repronex and Follistim, those expensive little creations which were intended to dupe Kiersten's body into thinking it was getting ready to be pregnant. We were back into our routine of fooling Mother Nature, baby-by-science in no time. I began to wonder how many more shots I'd have to administer to receive some kind of certificate in "prickery."

I accompanied Kiersten to her ultrasound checkups just as I had in the previous two rounds, but this time I was a little more comfortable with what I was seeing. The room was always the same—a monitor, a nurse, the good doctor, and the two of us, except I was still wearing my pants. Watching a virtual stranger stare up into your wife's most private of parts and insert what I liked to call the "in-vitro magic wand" could be a particularly unnerving experience. But I was a pro by now, and so was Kiersten. So I started to ask more detailed questions.

"What exactly are we checking for here again?"

"Well, we're making sure things are looking good in here…" Granderson replied as he manipulated the in-vitro magic wand with one hand, fiddled with a computer-mouse-like rolling ball with the other, and stared into the monitor admiring his dexterity.

"Eleven by eleven," he said to nurse Linda, who jotted down the information.

"So what qualifies as 'good' when you're looking around in there?"

"Well, you see this…" He moved the in-vitro magic wand and spun the cursor over several dark, oval objects on the screen. "That's an egg, that's an egg, that's an egg."

Hmm…you're good with that thing, Doc. If you hit her g-spot, though, I'm going to be pretty pissed.

"…and then here, see these three clear lines?"

"Yeah."

"That's the cervical lining. That's where the eggs will implant. We want to make sure the lining is nice and thick and these three lines are a good indicator."

"Wow. I feel like I should invite Kiersten to my colonoscopy now."

"In fact," he continued, unfazed, as he measured out the depth of the lining, muttering, "ten point two," which Linda promptly recorded, "…in fact, this is what I would characterize as Olympic-quality lining. It looks fabulous."

Kiersten looked over at me with a prideful smirk which declared, "I have Olympic lining!"

"I wonder what the television ratings are for that Olympic competition?"

I couldn't resist.

Again, using the rolling ball, he clicked and dragged a cursor across the screen, "Thirteen by eleven." Again, Linda dutifully recorded.

Granderson was particularly dexterous and enthusiastic about his ultrasounds. Watching his hand work that rolling ball and the wand, you really wouldn't be able to distinguish him from a grown man playing a game of Asteroids.

"I know I've asked you this before, but what are you recording again?"

"We're measuring the follicles," he answered with an eagerness suggesting that nobody else asked him these stupid questions.

"Is there some optimum size for an egg? Do you grade them single, double, and triple A?"

"Well, we're looking for follicles that have a rounder shape to them." He maneuvered the in-vitro magic wand again and pointed out three happy little dark spots on the screen. "Like these."

"Interesting…"

All the while, I could see Kiersten wasn't nearly as appreciative of my curiosity while she had her legs high in the air, paying good money to be molested. She flashed me a look that could either be interpreted as "Boy, aren't you Curious George today?" or "Shut the fuck up, you blathering idiot, does this look fun to you?"

I was sensing the latter.

"Twelve by fourteen," Granderson reported. Linda recorded with haste.

"So can you distinguish characteristics of the egg at this point outside of their general shape and size?"

Doc looked up over the sheet covering my wife's naked lower half. With the roller-ball hand, he adjusted his glasses and looked at me inquisitively. "Well, what are you looking for, exactly?"

"Can you tell which one of those would be left-handed with a plus-fastball?"

Kiersten's head turned to me. There was no mistaking which look this was.

"I think I'll wait outside. Carry on."

"Eleven by eleven, twelve by thirteen, ten by twelve…"

At least a dozen in there… things were looking good.

THE ROUTINE

I reached into the freezer and pulled out the icepack, handing it to Kiersten.

"What side did we do last night?" she asked.

"I can't remember, let me look at your back."

She pulled her shirt up and I tried to identify which welt looked more recently inflicted than the other. Her lower back was a battlefield of injection holes and bruises, each area about the size of a baseball, roughly three inches to the left or the right of her spine. This was where each rotating shot had to land, and it needed to be deep enough to reach muscle.

"I think it was your right side," I reported.

"Okay."

She started icing the left side in an effort to numb the skin enough to dull the pain of the injection.

I spent the next couple minutes laying out my materials.

I had a system by now—I collected my vial of sodium chloride, two vials of Repronex powder, the Follistim pen, the mixing needle, injection needle, and syringe. They were arranged in order, left to right.

"Where's the sharps container?" I asked.

The sharps container was a red plastic bin similar to the size of your average toaster—except this toaster had a bio-hazard sticker on it and was filled with used needles and vials of God-knows-what. It's common to find them in emergency rooms, but it was not your typical kitchen décor.

"It's on top of the refrigerator—remember, we put it up there to hide it from Anna when she stopped by?"

"Right, right…one of our close calls to revealing the big secret…"

I finished my preparations by getting the cotton ball and the alcohol swab ready. I stripped off the paper from a band-aid so it was ready to go in case there was blood. The last step was putting a saline solution pack into the microwave for post-shot comfort, heating it for three minutes.

1. Screw the mixing needle onto the syringe.

2. Draw up the sodium chloride.

3. Drain the sodium chloride into the Repronex. Make sure it dissolves completely.

4. Draw up the mixture, and repeat in the second vial of Repronex.

5. Draw up the mixture again.

"Damn it!" I piped up.

"What?"

"Oh, I drew it up without mixing in the stupid Follistim…"

5a. Drain the mixture back into the second vial of Repronex and extract the needle.

6. Inject 250 cc's of Follistim into the mix.

7. Draw the mixture back into the syringe.

8. Unscrew the mixing needle.

9. Screw on the injecting needle.

10. Rub the contents between your palms to warm it. Cold liquid inserted into the muscle hurts like hell.

11. Push the plunger on the syringe until a dab of liquid forms at the tip of the needle. Flick any air bubbles out of the syringe.

11a. Exude confidence.

12. Pick your spot on her back. Clean the area with the alcohol swab. Blow on it lightly to help it evaporate.

"Are you ready?"

"Yeah."

Go fast. Don't guide it in there, just stab. Quickly.

13. Insert the needle. Draw the syringe back a tiny bit to see if there's blood in the mixture. If there is, you've hit a vein and need to remove the needle and pick a new spot.

No blood. Good.

14. Empty the contents into her muscle. Remove the needle.

"Shit…this one's a bleeder."

"Don't let it get on my pants!"

"I've got it, I've got it…"

15. Press the cotton ball into the injection hole and cover with the Band-Aid. Press your hand firmly and massage.

16. Remove the bag of saline solution from the microwave, now hot, and hand it to Kiersten to hold on the affected area for comfort.

17. Throw what remains in the sharps container.

18. Offer a hug.

Repeat tomorrow at exactly the same time.

Making a child had never been so romantic.

BAREFOOT AND PREGNANT

Kiersten was raised Baptist, I was raised Catholic. I called myself a recovering Catholic, but despite that, my standard was that if there were drum risers in a church, I was out. If Jesus needed a kick drum in order for us to communicate with him, then I guess I was doomed to hell. That is, unless Dave Grohl was on drums; then not only would you have a great drummer, but you'd have one that looked a lot like Jesus. Again, I digress.

On the other end of the spectrum, Kiersten didn't want to mutter and drone through a solemn celebration of all the things we were doing wrong. Thus, we didn't attend church often. We once thought we had discovered a happy medium at one behemoth of a church until the pastor told a story about a woman who could never pay her bills, afford her rent, or generally make ends meet until she started to tithe—and then, you guessed it, her financial woes magically disappeared. While others clapped, hollered, and nodded, I laughed out loud, shook my head and held my hands over my face to disguise my disbelief. Although I vowed to never return, I'm not sure they would have let me back in.

Nonetheless, after many years of searching, we found common ground at a small Methodist church that was just a short walk down the street from our house. While we weren't regular attendees, this particular Sunday we were both uncharacteristically up early and figured it wouldn't hurt to give a nod to the big guy above.

This was a beautiful, historic, brick church complete with stunning stained-glass designs and an amazing display of floor-to-ceiling organ pipes flanked by giant gothic marble pillars, which acted as a backdrop for the altar. We enjoyed this church for a variety of reasons, but one in particular was how people from all perspectives were encouraged to just be themselves. The average age was probably somewhere in the mid-fifties—there weren't too many other young people, but that was okay with us.

One of the features of this church's services was an opportunity for parishioners to stand and share things they were particularly happy about or things they were particularly concerned about. Today, a well dressed gentleman in his early to mid-seventies, who bore a striking resemblance to Colonel Sanders, stood to speak.

"As you all know, I'm a political animal, and I have to say I'm concerned about something. With the recent appointment of another *conservative Catholic* to the Supreme Court, I'm concerned about the deterioration of our civil liberties at the hands of religious zealots." He said 'conservative Catholic' as if being Catholic was equivalent to being an evil puppy-kicking miscreant who stole lollipops from toddlers. As a recovering Catholic, I got a good chuckle out of it. He continued, "One of the fundamental tenets of our Republic, which makes this country such a great place to live, is freedom of religion. But freedom of religion includes freedom *from* religion. This administration and this court would rather have women back in the kitchen, baking cookies, barefoot, and pregnant!"

His speech was met with a polite smattering of applause.

Kiersten leaned over to me and whispered into my ear, "Where can I sign up for that?"

I started laughing out loud. Some people craned their necks and stared at me, wondering if I was a Catholic who had infiltrated the safety of their religious sanctum, and who found this amusing. Or maybe they thought I was the puppy-kicking, stealing-candy-from-a-baby type.

I regained my composure as quickly as I could. I actually gave the guy a ton of credit for his little diatribe—we needed more independent thinkers in this world. I also gave Kiersten equal credit for having a sense of humor throughout all of this.

I squeezed her hand and gave her a wink, still choking back my laughter. God, I loved her.

DINNER PARTY

It took us weeks of coordination to figure out retrieval and transfer days which we could take off. Kiersten always had to come up with some cockamamie illness since this wasn't considered to be truly "sick" leave, and I routinely had to tell my boss that Kiersten was having a "procedure" in order to be able to take adequate time off to care for her. I'm sure there was plenty of water-cooler talk about our mysterious time off—but there was no way they would have guessed IVF. Nobody does. It was just ridiculous, the dance that we had to endure in order to avoid telling our world about the situation we were in.

But after successfully negotiating our leave, the retrieval date arrived. As usual, we were late—mostly because neither of us could function without satisfying our oral fixation by way of coffee-associated paper cups and plastic lids. With decaf Americanos in hand, we rushed through the all-too-familiar clinic door ten minutes late under the disapproving stare of Granderson and the hopeful grandma-to-be.

Kiersten typically wore pajamas to the retrieval—after all, she would only impress people with what was on the inside today… literally. That's not to say she wasn't cute as hell with her pajamas on—it was just that your average adult wasn't typically seen in pink flannel flower print pajamas in public. As she was ushered back to the "chili dog" room, Ken came out with a pair of little blue booties and said, "You want to watch this one from the lab?"

To be clear, this was not typical. In fact, it was expressly against their policy. But because we had practically become their extended family (and of course, in the receptionist's case, direct family), Granderson and the gang extended me the offer of watching the retrieval from the other side of the infamous chili-dog room.

I wasn't immediately taken with the idea. I preferred not be in the way. With my luck, I'd wind up accidentally stepping on someone's triplets or inadvertently thawing someone before their time.

"Come on back, just put on some scrubs first," insisted Ken. "You'll have fun!"

How could I not take them up on this offer? It wasn't every day you got to see the retrieval of multiple human embryos in a lab. If you did, you were either a fertility specialist or had a much stranger life than mine.

"Okay, I'm in."

I walked down the hallway, glanced into the "collection room" and tried not to snicker like Beavis and Butthead might if they knew the dirty little things that happened in there. I hung a right past rows of four-foot tanks used in the cryogenic freezing process, and slipped into the laundry room, where I donned my scrubs. Looking in the mirror, I couldn't help but recite a few lines from

ER, calling to the nonexistent resident that we needed to "get a chest tube in this patient STAT!" Even though they look like the cheapest pajamas that you could buy at the local Wal-Mart, scrubs made you feel extraordinarily important.

I stopped in to see Kiersten as the anesthesiologist prepared to slip her into a waking coma.

"You look so cute in your scrubs, honey!" she said.

"Thanks. Maybe I'll see if I can keep them for some role-playing at home later..."

The anesthesiologist pretended he didn't hear that.

I kissed Kiersten on the forehead, told her I loved her, and was led into Ken's house of embryos, where kids ostensibly ate free.

The room was dimly lit and must have been at least 80 degrees. It couldn't have been more than twenty by twelve in size, but featured what appeared to be four half-sized refrigerators, multiple three-foot tanks which I was later told were filled with CO_2, and an incubator-like contraption straight out of *ET*, situated directly behind the chilidog window leading to the room where my wife's privates would be trolled for eggs by Granderson. In the corner I noticed a room-within-the-room that looked like a photographer's darkroom.

"Go ahead, go in there. That's where I do the ICSI fertilization," Ken said.

I opened the door. It felt like someone had stuck a blazing hair dryer in my face. I was reminded of being in Las Vegas in July when it was 119 degrees, except there was no porn lying on the ground, it didn't smell like garbage, and I wasn't drunk yet. But the heat was stifling.

"We have to keep it as warm as we can in there in order to mimic the temperature the embryos would experience in the body," Ken explained.

"So you're working in a life-sized womb here, huh?"

"Just shy of 100 degrees," he said proudly.

I couldn't help but think of all the inappropriate, though creative, ways I'd decorate the door if I were the embryologist. First on the agenda would be a giant vagina doorway. But I guess there was a reason God didn't make me an embryologist. My maturity level didn't allow for it.

About every two minutes, a machine kicked on—it reminded me of what an artificial respirator from about 1965 might sound like, a loud click with a sucking-then-hissing sound.

Click-whiirrrrr…

"That machine regulates the amount of Co2 in here," Ken explained, gesturing towards the *ET*-like incubator, "and in these refrigerators holding frozen embryos."

"Huh," I said in my best caveman imitation. This was all just too weird.

"A newer machine wouldn't make that noise—this one is pretty ancient. But a new one costs about $8,000, so I guess we can live with the noise for now," he said.

"Why Co2? I don't get it."

"When you breathe, your body is really managing the mixture of Co2 and oxygen —and that's what this machine is doing. It creates an environment that is similar to the one an embryo would have inside the body."

Click-whiirrrrr…

"That's pretty fascinating. So there are a bunch of frozen embryos in here?" I asked, gesturing to the refrigerators.

"Yep."

"Cool," I said, while actually thinking, *"Creepy!"* I recalled the scene in *The Matrix* where Neo was seeing the "real world" for the first time, staring out at the fields of humans grown like crops and kept alive in pods filled with goo.

The panel was lifted by Granderson on the other side of the glass window. It was apparently Go Time.

"Your chili-dog will be right up!" I said, to the delight of Ken and Granderson.

The scene was just surreal. An anesthesiologist to one side of Kiersten, monitoring her vitals, a nurse to her right, and Granderson in her... well... "down there." To his left was an ultrasound monitor. Visually, the scene looked very serious. But if you listened in, it sounded like a typical dinner party.

They talked about activities their kids participated in, exchanged stories about traffic and weather, even told a couple of off-color jokes. All the while, Granderson was inserting an apparatus into Kiersten's uterus, and by looking at the ultrasound monitor to his left, I could see him sucking the contents out of what were once her follicles into a large syringe, which he then handed back to Ken.

Click-whiirrrrr...

Ken took the syringe, emptied the contents into a glass dish and peered at the fluid through a high-powered microscope. He identified the eggs, separated them out, and put them into tiny glass tubes filled with pink-colored fluid.

"Overstock-dot-com," Kiersten blurted out.

The staff were quiet for a moment.

"Linda, did I tell you about the furniture I bought on Overstock.com?" asked Kiersten. Apparently, it was very common for people under anesthesia to talk through their surgery while they flirted with the brink of oblivion.

"No, you didn't."

"Oh, it's so cool. It's red leather. I bought two couches and a matching ottoman," she reported. Kiersten's speech was similar to that of someone who had imbibed a tad too much at a social gathering. Not belligerent, but not altogether articulate either, slurring one word into the next. In fact, the staff talked to her as if she were that moderately smashed guest—responding politely, but in a way that suggested they either didn't care or felt just a little sorry for her.

Watching the ultrasound monitor, I could see the tool Granderson was using to extract the eggs. Each penetrated follicle reacted as a bowl of Jell-O might if you pushed your finger into it—resisting at first, bending around the object pushing into it only to have the needle pop into it abruptly. The process was bizarre and amazing. I was watching this man extract eggs from my wife that would later be fertilized in the very lab I was standing in. This was how Kiersten and I would "make" a baby.

Granderson handed another large syringe full of fluid back through the window to Ken. Ken continued his search for eggs.

Click-whiirrrrr...

The conversation continued inside the room. The anesthesiologist talked about the school his children attended. Linda responded that she was familiar with that school and knew kids who had also gone there. Granderson. spoke highly of the place his kids attended.

"I'm working with a student who came from Montessori," said my drunken wife.

"You don't say?" one of the dinner party guests replied.

"Yeah, he's *waaayyyy* behind in reading," she asserted. "I don't really know what they did to him over there, but I did a reading test on him and he's not even at grade level yet, but he's a smart little boy so I'm sure I'll have him at standard in no time."

Inside the chili-dog room, I was imagining how horrified Kiersten would be if she knew she was doing this. But I was helpless. I couldn't do anything to stop her, so I just had to smile and continue to marvel at the whole situation.

"What's the score, Ken?" Granderson inquired.

"Seven," said Ken.

"What's seven—is that the number of eggs you have so far?" I asked.

"Yep. We haven't even gotten to her other side yet, either."

Click-whiirrrrr...

I heard Kiersten interrupt the conversation inside to ask, "Linda, did I tell you the joke that a co-worker told me?"

Oh, no. How can I stop her...

"Well, you know how Michael and I couldn't have sex for the last couple of weeks because of all this IVF stuff, right?"

Linda smiled and glanced in through the window at me. I could only shrug my shoulders. What could I do?

"Yes," Linda responded.

Okay, Mr. Anesthesiologist — time to hit her with a big dose!

"Well, she says that Michael is in the 'wolf position,'" Kiersten continued.

"The wolf position?" asked Linda.

"Yeah, he's on the ground, on all fours, howling at the cave to get inside!"

I covered my face.

The staff paused...then broke into laughter.

Kiersten giggled from her operating table.

I even yukked it up inside the chili-dog room.

All the while, Ken ignored what was going on, diligently searching for eggs inside the fluid Granderson continued to hand him.

Click-whiirrrrr...

"You want to come see this?" asked Ken.

"See what?"

"One of her eggs"

"I can't possibly mess it up?"

Ken laughed. "No... come over here and take a look."

As I looked through the microscope, Ken said, "You see that perfectly round little thing in the middle?"

"That's her egg?" I asked.

"That's her egg," he said.

This is so amazing, it's almost stupid. How many other husbands have stared at the egg that might be the beginning of their future child? This is absolutely insane.

"Wow. Just… wow…"

"What's the score, Ken?" asked Granderson.

"Eleven," he reported.

After a short time, the dinner party came to an end. Granderson. handed the last of the syringes back to Ken to sift through, and the anesthesiologist started to bring Kiersten out of her controlled state of unconsciousness. Granderson grabbed the chili- dog window panel and said, "Could you put the extra special sauce on those for me, Ken?" then closed up the room.

I thanked Ken for the opportunity to see what he does and headed back into the room to see Kiersten.

"How many did we get?" she asked.

"I think Ken said there were eleven."

"Eleven? That's it?"

"Remember, we're shooting for quality, not quantity this time."

"Okay. Did I say anything while I was out?" she asked.

"Well, yes. In fact, you really didn't stop talking the whole time."

"Oh, no… what did I say?"

"Well, you told everyone that joke that Julie told you."

"No I didn't."

"Yes you did."

"No…seriously? You're joking."

"I'm not."

"Oh, jeez…" she said remorsefully.

"Don't worry, babe—everyone thought it was hilarious. Are you feeling okay?"

"Yeah, I feel much better this time than I did last."

"Good to hear. Maybe that's a good sign."

There was a knock on the door. It was Ken, holding a little paper bag with which I was all too familiar.

"Michael, it's your turn…I think you know how this works."

I'd almost completely forgotten that he needed something to fertilize all of that hard work he'd done back in the lab.

I smiled and asked Ken, "Has anyone bothered to buy new magazines back there?"

"I doubt it. Sorry about that."

"Do you happen to have the underwear section from the JC Penney catalog?"

"I'm afraid not," he said.

I guess it's just me and Geena.

"I'd complain to the receptionist, but she's my mother-in-law, so there's not a whole hell of a lot I can do, is there?"

"Probably not…now go do your thing."

I kissed Kiersten on the cheek and headed out the door.

"Have fun!" she said.

Everyone gets such a kick out of the fact that I have to do this…

BLASTED

The evening after the 'dinner party' retrieval and my latest spicy rendezvous with the tormented davenport, Ken dialed my cell..

He was ultimately able to cull 12 eggs from the retrieval. This wasn't what we had been hoping for, as we were gunning for a couple dozen eggs, but it wasn't necessarily bad news, either. However, there was one initial issue.

"Only eight could be actually injected," he said.

"Is that normal, or was there some kind of problem with the fertilization process?" I asked.

"Well, I would have expected to be able to inject most, if not all of them, but some of the eggs weren't very responsive."

"Ken, I have no idea what that means, but I'll just accept that you did your best."

"I did."

"Good enough."

Ken continued with the less-than-ideal news. "Out of the eight that I could inject, six of them fertilized."

In my typical near-moron response, I asked, "Is that good?"

"Well, it's neither good nor bad. I've seen better, I've seen worse fertilization."

"How nondescript of you."

"Thanks, I'm getting good at that."

Wise guy...

The waiting game was on. It would take at least a couple of days before we heard about the status of the embryos. The plan was to transfer the "blast" embryos on day five, perhaps day six if they were a little bit slow in developing. On about day two, they'd determine if it would be necessary to freeze any fertilized embryos, assuming all were developing well.

About this time, Kiersten started to develop a headache. I assumed it was stress related, and in retrospect, it very well may have been. The headache escalated into a fever. She treated it with Tylenol and we both hoped it would remedy itself by morning.

Nothing doing. The next day, the fever was worse. She was nearing 101 degrees. We decided to take it easy for the day in hopes that it would run its course prior to the transfer day.

On the third day, we got a call from the clinic. Only three embryos had survived, but they looked good. We had two more days of waiting to see what we would have to transfer.

At this point, Kiersten and I were both disheartened. This was supposed to be the ringer round. The round where we had mini-superman and mini-superwoman embryos from which to choose. The round to end all rounds. Knowing we were down to *three* that looked "good" was demoralizing We were prepared for the worst on day five—that none of them would survive and we would be faced with some tough choices.

I decided that it was time for the clinic to call me directly, so that at least I could relay the bad news to Kiersten. The poor girl had been the recipient of so much bad news in the last year that she needed a break. I called the clinic and asked them to use my cell number for any further news.

Meanwhile, Kiersten's fever maintained at about 101 degrees, give or take a tenth. Nothing too worrying, but we couldn't figure out how to make it go away any faster.

On day five, I was dreading the phone call. Pessimism consumed me. The entire process was beginning to seem like a colossal waste of time and money. Kiersten and I joked about getting another dog, in addition to our moderately disobedient English bulldog, Bella, to satisfy our need for a kid. However, we hypothesized that twice the amount of canine flatulence could become a fire hazard.

We were both anxious to know what was going on at the clinic with our Day Five embryos, but our uncertainty about our future enabled us to discuss options.

"What are we going to do if this comes up with nothing?" she asked.

"Well, have lots of unprotected sex with confidence, that's for sure," I said.

We both get a chuckle out of it, sad as our situation might have been.

"Well, there's China. There's adoption. I'm beginning to feel like this is some kind of divine sign that we're destined to go the adoption route. I mean, how much longer are we going to ride this roller coaster?" she posited.

"Ah, an amusement park reference, thank you for putting it in terms I can understand."

"I'm being serious."

"I know, I apologize," I said. "You know I'm open to adoption. It's all part of 'The Plan,' right?"

"I thought you were apprehensive about the adoption process," she said. "Why the change of heart?"

"It's not a change of heart—I've always wanted to adopt. But I think being faced with the decision made me evaluate my values, and assess my understanding of what being a parent means."

"Like…" she queried, as if she was waiting for my punch line (such as, *"I'm just so looking forward to beating my kid,"* or *"Who will mow the lawn if we don't have kids?"* or *"I'll need someone to buy my Makers Mark when I can't drive anymore."*).

But, surprising even myself, I'd actually really thought about it.

"Like, is being a parent simply making a new life for the planet? Is being a parent unconditional love for someone just because she's got your DNA? What could possibly be more noble than giving opportunity to a kid who needs someone? How could I not love that kid like my own? I just don't get people who feel otherwise. I mean, just about anyone in the world can make a kid, and don't we know it. But it takes something more to open your life to someone who doesn't share your blood and call them son or daughter and provide for them the same opportunity you would give your own."

"Wow, you *have* been thinking about this," she said.

"I guess so. I just feel like people who don't understand adoption are so simple-minded. Maybe this is the outcome of months of IVF, maybe not—but this process has certainly confirmed my interest in adoption."

"So even if this were to work, you would want to adopt?" she asked.

"Absolutely."

It felt like progress.

*   *   *

My cell phone rang.

I reminded myself there had to be good news. This was our *third* round, I thought—statistically, we were in good shape. We'd be able to get on with our lives after this.

This round will work.

The phone rang...

This round is going to work.

The phone rang...

This round is working.

The phone rang...

Breathe.

I confidently answered the phone.

"Hello?"

"Michael, it's Ken."

"Yes sir...what's the plan?"

"Well, we've got nothing to transfer. None of the embryos have gone to blast."

Silence.

Uh... this round is NOT working.

"Nothing?" I said, despite the fact that I knew it sounded as if I either wasn't listening or was just slow.

Ken, in his best silver-lining speak, responded, "Well, one looks really good—it's compacting right now, it looks like it's about to go to blast."

"One looks good," I said, still reporting the obvious. I couldn't see anything more than a foot in front of me.

"Yes."

"What about the other two?"

"I'm not very optimistic about them. One looks okay, the other one doesn't look very good at all."

"What happens if they don't go to blast by day six?"

"That probably means that none of them are going to be viable."

"Viable meaning we won't transfer any of them, right?"

"Right."

"Well, that's just…that's just…super. Thanks for the call, Ken."

"Hang in there, man—we've still got a shot with that one."

"Thanks, Ken."

At least I got to diddle myself four times for this terrific news.

* * *

I had sequestered myself for the conversation with Ken so that Kiersten didn't have the fortune or misfortune of seeing my facial expressions or have to try and piece together the other half of the inaudible conversation, as she was known to readily do. I came back downstairs, passing our four bedrooms, three of them sitting idle, just waiting for occupants.

I found her huddled in front of a laptop, busying herself with some Dansko shoe pornography, and relayed the situation about our embryos, or lack thereof. We stared right through each other, expressionless, either pulverized by the disappointment, or in a mutual state of shock.

This was supposed to have been the last hurrah. Even if we wound up on the bad end of the statistical curve, we should have had lots of frozen embryos to use, and we wouldn't ever have to go through the stress of a retrieval again. It was just too painful to imagine that we'd have no shot at all after all of this. What would that mean? What did it say for our future chances? How could this be possible? Where was my Tanqueray?

Disbelief led to self doubt.

Self doubt led to anger.

Anger led to pure fucking rage.

Rage transitioned to sadness.

The sadness stuck around.

What a way to spend your vacation. Kiersten had to take a day off of work in case the embryos went to blast on day five. At least I could still go to work—I didn't have to have my employer hire someone to fill in for me as they obviously did with teachers. So here she was, it was 8:30 A.M. and she had just started her day with shitty, shitty, news.

I tried to think as quickly as I could.

"Why don't you go down to Dilly Dally?" I said.

Dilly Dally was an antique store about a half hour south of us of which we were both particularly fond. I thought the drive would be healthy quiet time, and could there be anything more cathartic than spending money on "stuff"?

She looked intrigued. I had to sweeten the pot.
"Buy whatever you want."
She grabbed her keys.

IT TAKES TWO TO TANGO

The clatter of gargantuan raindrops against our aging gutters woke me earlier than I would have liked. I tended to have inclement-weather-related anxiety when it came to our 100-year-old house, frequently depriving me of REM sleep. But today wouldn't be known for the weather, as it was "day six" in IVF-blast speak.

We peeled ourselves out of bed and attempted to go through our typical routine without breaking down from the stress. I was consumed with the overwhelming uncertainty of our situation. I couldn't stop wondering what the hell those fertilized embryos were doing.

Would they blast?

Would they fizzle out? If they did, where would that leave us?

Why did our embryos refuse to continue?

Why wouldn't they clean their room, for crying out loud?

Wait, I'm getting ahead of myself.

All the while, I was fighting the sense that our baby was due to be the antichrist. It was the only logical explanation for all of this. Don't think I haven't seen *The Omen*.

But as it was, neither of us could do a damned thing to affect the outcome of the news we were due to receive. It was either liberating or confounding. But we had to just carry on.

Go to work.

Business as usual.

Kiersten was even worse off, as her fever still persisted. 100 to 101.

I dug through the cabinets, searching for anything that could pass for breakfast. All I could find was uncooked brown rice, some sorry looking cashews, and preserves my aunt had given us for our wedding almost eight years ago. Very little on the food pyramid.

"So what are we doing?" Kiersten asked as I rummaged.

"I'm looking for the waitress. What are you doing?"

"What are we doing when we get nothing to transfer."

Oh, that "what are we doing."

"You don't know that we'll have nothing to transfer."

"It seems pretty likely."

Your pursuit of in-vitro Ms. Congeniality is officially over.

"Well, I don't know what we do. I might wind up getting really loaded tonight. Would you like to join me?"

"I might," she said.

That's the kind of spirit I like to see.

"I assume you're asking me what we'll do with this kid thing if we come up with nothing," I said.

"Yeah."

"I'm not sure if we should be making decisions about our future after we get this news," I suggested.

"Well, I think we should just go straight for adoption," she said. "I'm tired of waiting. I'm tired of the unknown. I'm tired of being let down."

"I don't blame you."

I was still volleying the idea of trying my aunt's preserves since I had just now learned it takes an hour to cook brown rice. Seriously, what the hell was with brown rice? Who has the time? But Kiersten's words made me stop to think for a moment.

You know what, why the hell NOT adopt at this point?

"Well, we're going to adopt one way or the other, correct?" I asked.

"That was the plan, except for the order."

"What stops us from modifying that plan?"

"I'm totally ready. This process is just ridiculous," she said.

My pocket started vibrating. It was Linda from the lab on my cell phone.

Honestly, who hasn't privately thanked the person who invented vibration for a ring?

I walked out of the room so Kiersten didn't see my face before I could tell her the news.

"Hello?"

"Michael, it's Linda. You have two to transfer."

I turned and looked at Kiersten, eyes wide with surprise, "We have two to transfer?!" I repeated, holding up two fingers.

Kiersten's jaw dropped.

"Yes, two to transfer," Linda said in a tone that seemed to ask, "Did I stutter?"

"Uh…wha…wow! Wow! Great! Two to transfer!"

"We need you here right away!" she said.

"We're out the door, Linda."

Shock…and…awe.

Turning to Kiersten, I was bewildered.

"Uh… I… Linda…" I sputtered.

"We have two?" she asked.

"We have two."

"I'm shocked. I'm totally shocked," she said.

"No kidding. Well, I guess I need to call in sick! Go change into your pajamas—we've got to run!"

Kiersten threw on her pajamas and we darted out the door as I called my office from my cell. I made up the best excuse I could, the usual vague line about Kiersten having a procedure. I knew nobody at work was buying that story anymore but I honestly couldn't care less—this was the most important thing in my life.

YOU GIVE ME FEVER

By 9:00 in the morning, we had two fertilized embryos firmly planted in Kiersten's uterus. This might not be your typical day, but it was becoming awfully familiar to us. We spent the next hour in the infamous chili-dog room, as per the usual post-transfer routine. Linda came in to tell us that our hour was up and we were free to go home.

"That was the absolute smoothest transfer I've ever seen," she said. "I have a really good feeling about this round."

Strangely, so did we.

Despite two titanic disappointments, although this round had not gone as planned, and in the face of the fact that we were completely prepared for the possibility that no viable embryos would even make it this far—now that there were two in there, we had hope. Hope, I'd learn, has the power to induce amnesia.

On the drive home, I made an optimistic stop at Starbucks. There was a big part of me that thought this would be our last round, and I could resume some degree of normal legal drug consumption in the form of my dose of caffeine. I got a triple tall Americano, but decided to get just two leaded shots and one decaf. No reason to go over-board. Yet.

"Can you feel my forehead?" Kiersten asked.

"Not feeling too hot?"

"No, I feel like my fever is back."

I felt her forehead, but I think I'm the single worst forehead fever feeler in history. I swear my Mother could feel my forehead and identify my temperature down to the hundredth of a degree. Me—I wouldn't know 60 from 160.

"I can't really tell. I'm pretty warm from this coffee. You could be a little warm, I'm not sure."

When we got home, Kiersten immediately stuck the thermometer in her mouth.

100.6 degrees.

"Well, you need to lay low for a couple of days any-way, so that should help your fever. Take an aspirin and just relax," I said.

Inside, I was concerned.

Why a fever? Why now? Can we just buy a break somewhere?

"Maybe it's just stress related," I said. "We've been through a lot emotionally in the last 48 hours. Get some rest and we'll see you how you feel tomorrow."

But the fever persisted.

For the next six days, weathering the daily shots, Kier-sten maintained a fever that fluctuated between 99 and 102 degrees, and there wasn't a whole hell of a lot that we could do about it. I tried to rationalize it by saying it was just God's way of "incubating the baby," but that ridicu-lous shit only lasted so long. We both knew this fever was bad news.

After days of uncomfortable progesterone shots in the ass and generally feeling like garbage, Kiersten decided to get her blood drawn a day early to see if she was pregnant. I had no objections.

She took the day off. I was at work, knowing that our future was being processed in some lab by people I didn't know. For some reason, I felt like they were playing a key role in whether or not we got a positive test, even though I knew the results had been long predetermined.

I couldn't shake the notion that the lab employees were incompetent.

I daydreamed about a team of nincompoops in their break room, wearing white lab coats, smoking cigarettes, playing poker, and belly-laughing to reruns of *Welcome Back Kotter*. They carelessly handled dozens of vials of blood. When the nurse arrived for results, they arbitrarily chose one, scribbled out "negative" or "positive" at random and handed the results to her. They broke out in collective laughter once the break-room door swung closed.

I became increasingly anxious.

Work began to seem trivial.

My thoughts were consumed by what might be. Our lives would change so fundamentally if she was pregnant. Our future would be so completely unclear if she was not. There was no middle ground, and I was about to find out which path it would be.

I closed the door to my office.

Along one of my office walls, I had a long antique mission-style bench. Nobody liked to sit on it because it was as uncomfortable as hell, but being the antique fan that I was, I thought it was pretty cool looking, so I kept it around. Today, it served a new function.

I dropped to my knees and prayed, using the bench as my pew

Whether it was an act of desperation or one of faith I don't know. But I was now begging God to help us. I didn't talk to the Big Man every day, but I was seriously calling in a favor this time. I was in the most dire emotional state that I could recall, and it was very foreign territory.

"Please God… please let this one work. Please give this to us. I'd say a Hail Mary or something, but I think I forgot it… and I don't want to try to fool you by saying the first few lines… because, after all, you're all-knowing and everything and you'll know I'm trying to pull the wool over your eyes… right? Okay, I'm getting off track… please, please, please… let this work. Kiersten deserves this. I don't know if we can take another setback, God. Please?" I audibly sighed. I couldn't even pray right.

This tension felt as if it was blinding me, like those strange occasions when you stand up too fast and your eyes momentarily blank and your body tingles. I felt my temperature climb and my heartbeat followed. I held my head in my hands. I didn't know if I should laugh, cry, or smash my head against the wall. I wondered to myself if I had ever been so emotionally fragile.

Adding to the strain, nobody around me could know what I was going through.

It was my quiet little secret.

It was my private hell.

And oh-my-God did I want a drink at that moment.

With my pathetic attempt at praying behind me, I opened the door back up and aimed to consume myself with some busywork that I'd been putting off for fear of not taking it seriously. I took a peek at the clock: 11:30. Close enough to noon, I figured—I clearly wasn't doing anything revolutionary at work—so I decided to take an early lunch and head home.

There I was free to traipse around my house and act like the complete nervous wreck that I was. I marched from room to room, talking to myself out loud, my very confused dog following me each step of the way.

I sat on our bed and stared at myself in the mirror. To my right was the Petunia Picklebottom diaper bag, crammed in a corner and covered in dust.

"What the hell are YOU looking at, Petunia Picklebottom!?"

Couldn't sit there.

My anxiety adventure brought me to the kitchen, and I figured it was a good time to exercise my right to have an adult beverage. If I continued like this, I was going to start scratching myself until I had open sores like some freaky meth-head. I think I saw that on *CSI-Miami* once.

Beer in hand, I took a pair of large swigs.

My eyes were closed as I swallowed.

I took a deep breath, inhaling the errant hop vapors in my mouth.

"You're losing your fucking mind," I said. My dog cocked her head sideways at me.

"You agree, don't you?"

Turned out, she just wanted some of my beer. I poured a little in her dish and gave her a pat while she lapped it up.

"Daddy's girl," I said.

I walked into the living room and sat down. In front of me was a frame that one of Kiersten's friends had given her, ostensibly because it looked old and would fit nicely with our 100-something-year-old house. The frame held a verse from the bible. I don't know if I'd seen it before or not, but as I began to read it, I started to cry. And cry. And cry some more. Soon, I couldn't even continue reading, my eyes blurred with unrelenting waterworks.

I should note that I'm fairly sure I could have been reading the ingredients to a box of Cheerios and had the same reaction.

I cracked.

I had bottled up all this emotion, all this frustration for the last ten months. I was supposed to be the strong one. After all, I wasn't the one with the ticking "clock." I'd never had visions of myself pregnant, a baby growing inside me. I was giving the shots, not receiving them. I wasn't artificially pumping hormones into my body. But sitting there, alone, I couldn't be the tough guy anymore. I couldn't even try to be funny. I just broke down into a blubbering, useless mess.

And then the phone rang. I was snapped back to the world of the hopeful.

"Hello."

"Hi honey," she said.

I couldn't identify the tone.

"Hi," I said tentatively.

"It's negative."

I ventured to open my mouth, but my brain misfired. Bupkis.

What is there left to say at this point?

What the fuck is going on?

I can't take this anymore... this might be it, our last shot.

"Are you okay?" she asked.

She asked *me* if *I* was okay.

"Not particularly. What about you?"

I could hear her lose her composure. Her voice cracked as she said she couldn't talk about it right now.

"Come home," I said.

She hung up.

I felt all sense of hope evaporate.

Staring out my front door, I was lost.

I had no idea why this was happening to us and there wasn't a fucking thing I could do to fix it.

I just stood there, gazing aimlessly at the landscape in front of me. All I could feel was complete emptiness.

I can't tell you if genius is hereditary because heaven has granted me no offspring.

– James Whistler (1834-1903)

DINNER, UP WITH OLIVES

It was roughly 4:00 and we had both received news that we weren't sure how to rationalize. We were adults dealing with adult decisions we couldn't believe we were being forced to make. Instead of talking it out, we approached our problems, once again, with our stomachs.

"Is there anything I can do?" I asked.

"We could order Sam's," she said.

"Seriously!?"

"Yes. I'm hungry. I want Sam's."

"No way in hell am I going to let you go in there and face the 'why no baby' barrage!"

"Well, just order and pick it up for me. Please?"

How could I say no?

I grabbed my cell—the New Peking Restaurant was programmed into my phone, of course. I even knew the fast-dial digits I could hit to get them on the horn quicker. Jessica answered, and I ordered up the usual: Mongolian Beef, pot stickers, and extra rice. I could feel my cholesterol rise just by saying it.

"TEN MINUTES IS READY!" said Jessica.

Hmm…ten minutes.

Ten minutes gave me enough time to go to the liquor store to buy a bottle of Tanqueray on the way to picking up dinner. I needed a martini…and there was no damned well-intentioned physician who could tell me that it wasn't good for me to do so right now because despite all of our efforts, we were still in the same miserable situation we were in a year ago when all this started.

And I *needed* a martini.

"Be back in a few," I said, and darted out the door.

I arrived at the liquor store and noticed a parking spot directly in front of the shop.

"Rock star parking!" I said out loud, a toothy grin escaping my otherwise stoic exterior.

Putting the car in park, I turned and pulled the key out of the ignition.

And then I hesitated.

I was fixated on the individuals entering and exiting the store, frozen as I watched the parade of clowns of questionable character come and go. I couldn't shake off the notion that I shouldn't be there.

What if there's another round? What if that is the round that will work—but only if you continue to avoid liquor?

"Shit."

I could literally see the shiny green bottle on the back wall from my parking spot.

Is it worth it? What if you do another round and it doesn't work again, but you've gone on a bender? Will you always wonder 'what if'?

"Fuck."

All I really wanted out of life at that very moment was a simple little martini. And I knew I couldn't have it.

"NO, NO, NO, SHIT, SHIT, SHIT!!!" I yelled as I physically abused my steering wheel. A patron noticed my little tirade and looked at me inquisitively. The kind of look that hovered between "should I ask him if he needs help" and "should I call the police."

Okay, now you look completely pathetic. Screw you, pal, I've got low motility.

I started the car and got out of there. I needed to get to the New Peking before our dinner got cold.

As I entered the restaurant, Jessica was at the front desk. I wondered what we would chat about now that Kiersten had put the kibosh on kid talk.

"OH, HI MIKE!"

"Hi… how are you?"

"GOOD, GOOD — YOU HAVE BABY?"

Perfect. Sodium induced memory loss.

"Uh…no. No baby. Pot stickers will do for now."

"OH, NO BABY? WHY NO BABY?"

"We just like to torment you and Sam," I said.

Can I get a side of shotgun-to-kill-myself-with, if it's no bother?

Jessica stepped aside and began to fill a to-go bag with our order.

Her five year old child, Brianna, popped her head up from behind the desk and startled me. But, my God, she was cute.

"Oh! Hi there! How are you?" I asked.

She smiled at me sheepishly and ducked back behind the counter.

Jessica spoke to her in what I could only surmise was Mandarin. Again, I'm not a native speaker…cut me some slack.

Brianna re-emerged from behind the counter.

"I'm FIVE," she said.

"Wow! I remember you when you were just a baby." I gestured with my palm down low, as if that were the international symbol for baby.

She turned to Jessica and said something. They exchanged words.

"I DON'T KNOW, SOME PEOPLE NO WANT BABY!" Jessica said to her.

What the hell?

"I DON'T KNOW, SOME PEOPLE NO LIKE BABY!" she continued.

The kid is in on this act now? Just poison the Mongolian Beef and put me out of my misery, for crying out loud.

"IS OKAY, NOT EVERYONE LIKE BABY!"

Brianna looked back at me, perplexed.

Yeah, hi, little girl—I no like baby. I've just been trying to have one for the last year to no avail and your parents mock me every time I come in here.

She smiled at me, one front tooth missing, and disappeared back behind the counter.

As painfully ironic as the whole exchange was, I could only grin wryly. I couldn't even believe I was witnessing this with what we'd been through today. It was just *perfect.*

Sam emerged from the kitchen.

"Mike! I knew was you—Mongolian Beef and pot sticker!" he said.

"Yeah, you've got us hooked—we're Mongolian beef addicts and you're our dealer!"

"Ah, yes, yes! You have baby?"

Smooth transition, Sam.

"No, no baby, Sam."

"Oh, you want borrow my baby? Maybe you like? Maybe you have one of your own?"

Breanna popped up, pushed her cheeks together, squished her face with her hands and subsequently burst out laughing.

She was truly adorable.

For a moment, I thought, *yeah, I'll take you up on that.* But I couldn't help looking at her and wondering if we should just adopt. Here was a beautiful little girl, and Kiersten and I both knew we wanted to adopt—and we both knew there were hundreds of abandoned little girls in China while we battled with our unknown inability to procreate.

Why stick to our plan? The plan seems idiotic now.

Why do we need a biological kid before we adopt? Why not now?

"Generous offer, Sam, but I'll just take dinner for now," I said.

"Okay, okay—I give you extra rice, no charge."

"You're good to your junkies, Sam! Thank you!"

As I arrived home, I realized thirty minutes had somehow transpired.

"Where have you been?" Kiersten asked.

"Well, I went to the liquor store."

"Where's the liquor?"

"Kind of a long story…but I have to tell you about Sam's," I said.

I recounted my experience and we both had a healthy guffaw about the absurdity of it all. It was nice to enjoy each other's company for a moment without thinking about the gravity of the news we had received just hours earlier. We were completely uncertain about our future, but sodium-rich Cantonese food helped us put that aside at least for a day.

FNB

I was awakened prematurely—partly because my left leg was asleep and partly because I couldn't stand the snoring any longer. Bella, our English bulldog, was responsible for both. She was draped across my knees and snoring louder than I could even venture to imitate. It was almost cartoonish—like a combination of a country farmer firing up a pea-vine tractor and Paul Bunyan snorting back some phlegm.

It was Saturday morning. Bella was allowed to sleep with us to provide some moral support and some comic relief. She was a pretty intuitive dog—she could tell when we needed her to be cute and cuddly. Unfortunately, it usually meant I got little sleep, so it was a rare occurrence for her to sleep with us during the work week. Bella gave new definition to "bed hog," and with all the snoring, she almost resembled one as well. At 65 robust pounds, it was like sleeping with a restless, drooling, gassy, snoring sack of concrete. Somehow, Kiersten was always able to block her out.

I willed myself to sit up, get out of bed and imitate some yoga stretch I think I once saw on a commercial. My eyes felt like they were sunk a foot into my skull and I had the energy of a clinically depressed koala bear. Looking to my right, I saw the long neglected 'Fond of Flora' diaper bag covered in months of dust. "Petunia freaking Pickle-bottom… what the hell do you think you're looking at," I mumbled as I shuffled to the bathroom.

Staring at myself in the mirror, I could see the effects of a year's worth of stress on my face. "Nice bags," I said. It seemed I was starting to look more and more like my bull-dog.

I decided to make a list of things to do today to keep us relatively busy. An idle Saturday after a failed third round sounded too depressing. So I tried to fill our day with distractions.

1. Coffee
2. Haircut
3. Shop for clothes we don't need
4. Shop for furniture we don't need
5. Shop for tile that we sort of need
6. Eat out someplace particularly bad for us

I let Kiersten sleep in until about 10:30, at which point we finally headed out to get some coffee. I decided to get a little bit of caffeine in mine and Kiersten sinfully went for the latte over the Americano, but it was well deserved. We sat outside with our sunglasses on so we could stare at people anonymously. Watching the downtown shoppers scurry about like purposeful ants armed with AmEx, we sipped our coffee and chatted about the weather. Mindless and pleasant. I was optimistic about today. But then again, I was often rather buoyant when consuming my filtered friend in a paper cup.

As we finished our coffee, both of us slumped down in somewhat comfortable aluminum patio furniture with our feet extended leisurely, a woman pushed a stroller by. It was a double stroller. One kid was probably two, the other had likely joined us a few weeks ago. Dad followed with another on his shoulders.

Roughly two minutes passed, neither of us saying a word. I could feel Kiersten's angst. She wasn't saying anything to avoid sounding bitter. She was trying to repress the negative. Her resentment was palpable. I decided to give it an outlet.

"Fucking normal breeders," I said.

Kiersten spewed a few ounces of latte across the sidewalk as she laughed.

It was good that we could find some humor in this, because our day couldn't have turned out more ironically twisted.

Across town, Kiersten dropped me off for my haircut. She was going to do some grocery shopping while I had my locks trimmed. It was one of those chop-shops where you didn't need an appointment and you were really never sure how you'd look when you left—but I wasn't nearly vain enough to give a shit about my hair, so the price was right.

A young woman approached the front and said she could take me back. She was probably 19. Maybe 20. And she was so pregnant, I'd swear she had the whole cast of Cirque de Soleil in her belly.

"So, do you know what you're having?" I asked. She probably thought I was talking about gender, but I was really wondering if it was human.

"No, we're not finding out the sex—but my boyfriend thinks it's a girl."

Your boyfriend. Perfect.

She hacked away a good portion of my hair and asked me what I thought.

"Tough to make me pretty, but you did your best," I said. I needed to escape before Kiersten saw who was cutting my hair. *I'll get out of here early and flag her down in the parking lot,* I thought.

As I met my expecting hairstylist at the register, I turned to discover Kiersten walking up from the parking lot. I waved my index finger in the air and mouthed, "*Just a minute,*" thinking maybe she'd just go back to the car or wait outside.

But she didn't. I couldn't stop her. It occurred to me that we needed to take American Sign Language courses together.

She entered, tousled my hair, and then saw the woman who might very well be carrying a brown bear in her womb. She looked at me with disgust.

"Her boyfriend thinks it's a girl," I said with a smirk.

Kiersten's face was expressionless save for the inferno in her pretty blue eyes. If she could speak, I knew what she'd say.

Fucking normal breeders.

We scuttled out of there and headed out to do some shopping. Our first stop was a local furniture retailer with a great mix of hip/retro furniture. We browsed around and oohed and ahhed at some of the items for sale. We never tired of looking at furniture, even if we didn't really "need" anything.

"Can I help you find anything in particular?" asked the young female shop owner.

You guessed it—one in the oven.

We were both pulverized by the repeated painful irony. I imagined that God was laughing at us right now. At least I hoped he was. Otherwise, this was truly perverse.

"Oh, just browsing," I said. "You've got some great stuff here."

"Thanks—if you need anything, don't hesitate to ask," she said.

As she walked away, I whispered to Kiersten, "How about telling us how you did *that*," gesturing to her belly.

Kiersten laughed. It wasn't a belly laugh nor was it a cackle, but it was more than just a courtesy laugh—maybe a chuckle.

Mission accomplished.

* * *

Walking back to the car, we laughed about our day. We laughed to help us keep from crying. To try and mask the pain. Or maybe it was my haircut. It could definitely have been the haircut.

Kiersten settled into the passenger seat and discovered a message on her cell.

"My mother called," she said.

"Let me guess—she's pregnant."

"Granderson wants to talk to us about options," she reported.

Options. Options…What options could possibly be left? Inject testosterone into my scrotum?

"I think they want to test your boys."

Test? Haven't we already tested?

"Frankly, I'm not sure they're ready for the SAT, it has been a tough year on them —and from what I can tell from their labs, they're all ADD, so we'll need extra time on our tests. Now, I'll need about 23 million #2 pencils to start with…"

"Clever," she said, unimpressed.

My humor is so wasted on our current plight.

"What kind of test? Haven't we already established what my boys are capable of?" I asked.

"Apparently, it's some kind of DNA test."

DNA? Mulder, you've got to come take a look at this …

"This isn't going to involve any bone-marrow removal or anything, is it?"

"I doubt it," she said.

Phew.

"Seriously, what have you heard from your mom?"

"Apparently, there's some kind of test that they can do on your sperm to identify if there are issues with your DNA. I guess it's very new technology—called a 'fragmentation test'—but they can pretty much pinpoint the issue to a DNA problem if they see certain characteristics in the sperm DNA."

"Wow—now that's heavy," I said.

"No kidding."

"Well, what's the plan—when are we going in?" I asked.

"He wants to see us right away, but I don't think I can meet with him. I just can't go in there right now. It's too soon—I'll just… I don't know what I'll…"

"It's fine, Kiersten—I can go by myself and talk to him. You don't need to go. I promise I'll pay attention—I'll let you know what he says."

No reason for Kiersten to have to go back into the shop, look at all of the pictures that successful IVF couples send of their kids, hear the fourth iteration of it-will-work-the-next-time tidings from the staff, listen to Doc describe some of the desperate measures to which we might have to resort in order to conclude this baby chase.

While I feared visiting Granderson without her (how could I possibly ask all the right questions like she would?), I knew I had to do it. So I called the clinic and made an appointment as soon as possible.

If your parents never had children,
chances are you won't, either.

– Dick Cavett

SOME PEOPLE

I wasn't altogether sure if there was a DNA-fragmentation-test reason for eating dinner out, but I made a note to myself to check the Frivolous Spenders' Handbook to verify. I was sure it'd be reason 5,000 or so, but I could guarantee it included consuming beer.

We planned a dinner with friends who happened to be among the few who knew of our recent struggles with infertility. The first painful reality was that our dinner plans were at the North Fork Brewery and I couldn't take full advantage of their specialty. But if I could choose three places where I would happily die, the North Fork Brewery would most definitely be on the list.

This was more than just a brewery with tremendous craft beer of overwhelming strength and depth; it was also a pizzeria featuring thin-crust New York-style pizza which was simply fabulous. But that wasn't all; you could also get married there. Indeed, it was also a wedding chapel, although none of us knew who performed the services or where the chapel was. I think the whole purpose of the wedding chapel was for those who sampled each and every available beer, got loaded, fell in love, and couldn't afford the trip to Vegas. Who were we to judge?

The location couldn't have been any more remote. It was buried in the forest, located off of a treacherous two-lane highway which took most drivers to a popular skiing destination to the east, and all the county folk back to town going west. You could always discern the visitors to the North Fork because only regulars knew how to anticipate the turn into the parking lot off of a 55-mph highway in the pitch dark around a blind corner. The building itself looked like a glorified Unabomber shack with a gravel lot. They weren't much for aesthetics. But oh, could they make beer.

Fortunately, I had planned ahead and had a beer "banked" for this particular occasion. Even if I hadn't, I think I would have lied. If Susan found out, maybe I'd just have her killed.

The second unfortunate reality was our discovery that our dinner dates were also dealing with the fickle nature of baby-making. They'd tried to conceive for several months to no avail, and were beginning to take more interest in the goings-on of our plight than they had in the past. Kiersten and I both prayed that they wouldn't face what we had, but it was obviously out of our hands. I took joy in relating stories of Sam's to them, particularly the last encounter regarding 'why no baby.'

We sat down and ordered as much pizza as we could possibly imagine eating and then two of us ordered a beer. Before making a decision, I scanned the brewery's beverage menu. I imagined drinking their porter. I literally closed my eyes, visualizing the consumption of their IPA. I think I probably smacked my lips and licked at my imaginary pint glass rim. But in the end, I couldn't possibly resist ordering their barley wine. Despite the fact that they served it in a ten-oz. glass, it would be my beer of the week and I'd be eternally grateful that I had ordered it. It was that good.

While the four of us enjoyed the outstanding beer and pizza, we also shared frustrations regarding our unsuccessful attempts at procreation and the seemingly unpredictable nature of kid production. There was something particularly liberating about being with another couple who could truly relate to our situation without feigned concern or, worse yet, pity.

We were finishing up our dinner when I noticed one of Kiersten's former co-workers get up to leave her table and start to exit. This was a woman who, along with another broom-riding wench, had tortured Kiersten with unending antagonism at a previous job. The bullying not only caused Kiersten to leave her place of employment, but occasioned a year's worth of therapy to help her deal with the callous nature of a pair of young teachers who had been downright evil to her, taking advantage of her generosity towards others. This particular individual, however, remained consistently oblivious to the situation and often treated us like we were all old chums.

"Oh, hi, you two," she said.

"Hi," I replied unenthusiastically, trying my best to burn holes in her skull with my narrowed, piercing stare.

"Don't you just love the food here?" she asked.

All four of us smiled and nodded methodically, hoping that she would just leave it at that and go away. But she didn't.

"So, do you two have any kids yet?" she asked, holding the hand of her six-year- old.

Oh, fuck you. Wrong table to ask, lady…

All four of us just looked around at each other, wondering who would have the diplomacy to fend off her question or the balls to tell her to shove one of the beer pints right up her ass.

I spouted the first response in my head.

"Well, some people no like baby."

My table erupted with laughter.

She left without an explanation, bewildered.

Power in numbers.

Strength in Sam's wisdom.

TIPPING POINT

As I drove to the appointment with Granderson to discuss options, and apparently my *friggin'* DNA, my
thoughts ran faster than I could process them. Every avenue in my head seemed to lead to the same destination:
How could this be our situation? How could our ability to
do something so innate be so completely inconceivable?
Why us?

My ability to laugh all of this off had entirely eroded in
the last 24 hours.

I began to get anxious. I squirmed around the cab of
my truck, uncomfortable in my own skin, seething like a
heroin addict needing a fix.

I could feel my blood pressure rising.

I was angry.

Very angry.

Sam Kinison angry.

I needed an outlet, and unfortunately, I was behind the
wheel of a 1977 Ford full-size pickup with a 480-cc V8 engine under the hood. This was a giant, thundering truck
and I could inflict some serious damage if I was so inclined... and did I ever feel inclined.

I had been trying to keep my emotions in check for the last several months, but I was growing increasingly hostile and everything around me was making it worse. I felt as if I were the reincarnation of Michael Douglas stuck on the freeway in *Falling Down*.

I'm driving to an appointment to talk about having the DNA of my sperm tested for abnormalities.

How is this our reality?

What the hell have we done to deserve this?

I had reached a boiling point.

All the ridiculous, insignificant stupid shit that people do began setting me off.

For starters, the car in front of me sported a window sticker of a mischievous Calvin-like character urinating on a Chevy symbol. I'm sure you've seen it. The man was driving a Dodge truck. Clever, right?

Chevys urinating on Fords; GMC trucks on Dodge trucks. Honestly, who really gave a rat's ass what kind of truck anyone drove? I'm going to market a new sticker that features Mother Earth pissing on a giant truck with a caption that reads, "Back at you."

I noticed there was a baby seat next to the driver.

Perfect. This jackass is a father. His family tree probably has so few branches it's more like a family stick, and yet he can make a baby anytime he wants.

I wondered to myself if we could somehow rid the planet of everyone with a window sticker featuring the mischievous Calvin-like critter… a moron-cleansing of sorts, in which they would all be killed by being strapped to the chairs of an auditorium where Celine Dion entertained them until they either died of shock or starved, whichever came first.

Maybe I'd run for office on that platform.

Sitting at the light that never seemed to want to change, I noticed another unsavory creature to my right. He was talking on his top-of-the-line, so-thin-you-could-barely-see-it cell phone, window down, sunglasses on despite overcast skies, music blaring. I speculated that he wasn't really talking to anyone, he was just that insecure about himself. He drove some sort of ridiculously expensive Mercedes. Only his hair and fu-manchu were more meticulously manicured than the black leather interior or the glisten of his aftermarket chrome wheels.

I stared at him with about as much contempt for another human being as I hope to ever feel. Then he casually flipped his cigarette onto the street.

I fantasized about climbing out of my truck, grabbing his wayward Marlboro Light and grinding the hot coals across his Italian leather bucket seats. I imagined the expletives he'd use to describe me, my mother, and my crappy truck, while I remained utterly unfazed.

I smiled, just a little.

In my current state, even my directional signal was a target. As I sat at this cursed light that REFUSED TO CHANGE, my left turn signal seemed particularly audible. It blinked with a perfect, irritating rhythm. The clicking noise seemed to become louder with each flash, goading me into a frenzy.

Click click

Click click!

CLICK CLICK!

I wanted to destroy the light which was responsible for this. I daydreamed about forcing my hand through the dash and ripping the cord back through the steering wheel, ignoring the blood cascading down my forearm like I was a cool Kurt Russell in some hipster-retro Quentin Tarantino flick.

I was dangerously angry and the last place I needed to be was behind the wheel of a gigantic rig.

Fortunately for me, my truck, and everyone surrounding the two of us, this evil, foul, ill-timed traffic light finally changed and I promptly arrived at the clinic.

I gave myself a pep talk in the parking lot to pull myself together.

You've got to get through this. Kiersten is relying on you... don't blow this. Pull it together. Just leave this anger in the cab—deal with it when you get back.

SOUTH DAKOTA SPECIAL

Doc shook my hand.

"What are we going to do with you guys?" he asked.

"I'm not sure. It's illegal to buy children on eBay, right?"

"Well, I think we're going to be able to get you one regardless... come on in," he said.

I was escorted into the room where I had almost fainted nearly a year ago. A lime-green-and-pink floral patterned couch was flanked by the modern roll-top desk that was so tidy with neat piles of paper, magazines and pens, it almost appeared staged. Doc always sat on the desk chair, with patients relegated to the couch, where you sat about a foot lower than the good doctor, and therefore felt both 12 years old and about four feet two inches.

I despised this room.

I was inclined to just stand through the meeting, but Doc's eyes implicitly gestured me towards the couch as if he was using the power of the MD to get me to plop my ass down. I acquiesced and squished morbidly into the cushion.

"We were all pretty surprised with the last round—we thought we had a pretty good chance with those embryos," he said.

"Yeah, I know the feeling."

"I still feel like it's a matter of 'when' and not 'if' with you two. We just haven't had the right mix of science and luck."

"I guess that's good news. Where does this put us?" I asked.

"Well, you could try another round the way you've been doing it—perhaps with a couple of tweaks…"

"Tweaks—like changes to her drug regimen?" I asked.

"Yes."

Such insightful questions—Kiersten would be so proud.

"Or you could entertain the possibility of using donors to help you, if we turn up more problems," Granderson said.

Donors—like rich people paying for more rounds of in-vitro for us?

"You're talking donor egg or donor sperm, right?" I asked.

"Well, good question," he said.

I'm channeling Kiersten's inquiries…

Doc continued, "It could be sperm or egg or perhaps even both."

"And what's going to tell us which of those options we're looking at?"

"We're at a point where we need to start eliminating some questions." he said.

"Such as?" I inquired.

"Well, we'd like to have your sperm tested."

"Yeah, Kiersten told me something about a DNA test, but I don't know much else."

"There's a company in South Dakota that can do what's called a DNA fragmentation test, which will allow us to see the quality of the DNA of your sperm."

I'm going to send my sperm to South Dakota?

I was intrigued by this DNA test technology, but I was still troubled by the fact that this practice took place in South Dakota. I figured the most notable collection in Rapid City was the Custer State Park Buffalo roundup, not an assortment of thousands of genetically challenged sperm samples.

"Tell me a little more about this test," I asked.

"Well, you know how DNA has a helix, like a twisted ladder," Granderson began, grabbing his pencil and paper.

"You really don't have to draw me a picture, I've got the mental image..."

"Well, some sperm have DNA where the helix is frayed and in some cases, the ladder portion is actually broken. This helps us to establish whether or not the problem is the sperm."

Now that's fascinating.

As stunned as I was about the situation I was in, I was amazed by the technology. It was difficult enough to fathom someone looking at my little swimmers to begin with, let alone doing some kind of analysis of their actual DNA makeup. I could only imagine how much time and money this could save many couples who wouldn't otherwise know early on what the problem was.

He continued, "So we'd need you to leave a sample here, then we have a special container that we'll send it in, and we can have the results typically within a week."

What a fun little vacation for my boys…

"Fine with me. Sign me up." A moment later, I asked, "So what happens if this thing comes back and it says my sperm DNA is all messed up?"

"Look—the fact of the matter is, if you want to start a family, I can give you one. If your DNA test comes back and it tells us that your sperm is the problem, then we need to start looking at new options."

I'd file that assessment under 'nebulous.'

"Do you ever run out of options around here?" I asked.

"Not really."

"So what kind of options are you suggesting?"

"Well, there's the donor option."

"I'm not losing an organ, am I?"

"Donor sperm, Michael," he said.

Oh, right— that kind of donor.

"And if the DNA test comes back and shows there's no fragmentation?" I asked.

"Well, we may want to explore the possibility of donor egg then. Or perhaps donors for both the sperm and the egg…"

I was hanging in there pretty well during the DNA thing, but the donor stuff was beginning to freak the shit out of me…

"…but we can talk about that after we get the DNA test back." he said.

Pull up a comfy chair as I recap:

There I sat, alone, in the room where I had nearly tossed my cookies roughly one year ago when I heard that there was some kind of issue with our ability to naturally procreate. Since then, we had undergone three rounds of in-vitro fertilization. I'd had to repeatedly jerk off in a hyper-sterile room with crummy pornography as "inspiration," while my mother-in-law sat outside. I suffered through caffeine withdrawals; I'd practically quit drinking altogether, which alienated me from, well… myself. My wife had been violated like she was a 1974 Volvo donated to the technical college for first- year transmission students. Our kitchen doubled as a pharmacy. She had endured months of daily injections from me, which may or may not have been in a vicinity in which they belonged. We had filled three 'Sharps' containers with needles, syringes, vials of drugs and other sundry materials. We'd lived two lives for a year, one representing the world we projected and the other representing the one we actually inhabited. And now I had just heard that I was sending my boys to South freaking Dakota so that they could peer in at the twisted little ladders of my DNA. It might or might not be completely wrecked, and depending on the outcome, we might be having a fun-filled conversation about using the product of someone else's collection room extravaganza or some complete stranger's eggs to imitate a natural biological pregnancy.

I lingered a moment, digesting the information. I was hunching forward on the couch, elbows on both of my knees, my left hand massaging my forehead. I was grinning ever so slightly. This situation was just so absurd, I couldn't help but find humor in it.

But I was out of insightful questions. I was devoid of my typical sarcasm. No wit in sight. I was so utterly confused, I was numb to this revelation of the human genome project to be conducted on my sperm, for all I knew in some secret lab on Mount Rushmore.

"Kiersten might be done," I blurted out.

"Done?"

"Yeah, I don't know if she'll go for another round or any of this donor business."

"Well, I don't think this is the time for either of you to make decisions. I'll say it again—if you want to start a family, I can make that happen for you. Let's just see what this test says and we'll go from there."

I thought about how his definition of a family was probably different than mine. Some Frankenstein lab baby mixed together with what's-his-face's sperm and so-and-so's eggs felt like a much stranger proposition than adopting at this moment. But I suppose just because someone else's kid comes out of your uterus doesn't make it much different than adoption, does it? Kiersten would argue the benefits of vaginal integrity. Regardless, Doc was probably right—I'd reserve judgment right now. This had been one hell of a day and I should just fold up tent and run before it got any stranger.

"Well, Doc, that's about all I can stand…"

"Okay then—please call if you have any questions; you know we're here for you guys."

"I appreciate that—you've been great, thank you."

On a positive note, I exited the dreaded almost-puked room, and made my way past the front desk towards the door.

"Oh, Michael Charles!" said my mother-in-law in an excited soprano tone, saying the two names so quickly, they practically become one. *MICHAELCHARLES!* She almost always called me by my first and middle name. In fact, after a while, even some of the other staff members started calling me Michael Charles. I took it as a term of endearment, despite the fact that it felt a little condescending coming from anyone but my mother-in-law, Karen.

"Yes?"

"We need to schedule your appointment."

"Can I call in when I have my calendar in front of me?"

"Oh, of course," she said.

"Thanks."

I took a step to leave.

"Oh, um…Michael…um…I'm not sure what your uh…"

She started turning red.

This is going to be bad.

"Well, I'm not sure how to, er… what you and Kiersten have…um…"

"Just say it," I begged.

"…what your *abstinence* schedule looks like…but you can't have…uh, you can't…well…you need to be abstinent for at least three days before the test," she stuttered.

How many other people have had the good fortune to speak clinically to their mother-in-law about when they could or couldn't have sex with her firstborn?

"Well, I'm not sure what my abstinence schedule looks like either…but I'll call when I do."

What a perfect punctuation to my afternoon.

I exemplified an unceremonious exit.

*   *   *

I left my appointment no more content than when I had arrived. I continued to wonder, why me? Why us? Seriously, my DNA? How could this possibly be our situation? And where's my drink?

I slid back behind the wheel of my monstrous 70s-era beast of a truck, greeted the hostility I had left there roughly an hour earlier, fired up the engine and roared out of the parking lot with a demonstrable degree of aggression.

Three fucking rounds of IVF and now I'm doing a DNA test on my sperm while everyone around us cranks out kids and half of them are an accident.

This meeting hadn't brought me to a peaceful place. I wondered to myself if Kiersten would be better off with someone else.

Should I have never married her? If I have this DNA test and it comes out that my boys are freaky little DNA mutants, what good am I? Isn't this the purpose of being a man — to be able to make babies? If this test comes back bad, what will I do? How can I deal with this knowing that I'm the cause?

I made a left and had to slow down as traffic backed up. There were cars everywhere.

"What the...what now?" I said out loud to all of the angry little people inside the cab of my truck.

All I wanted at that point was a pint of very strong India Pale Ale. Ok, two. No, three.

There was a throng of black-clad individuals flowing towards the Greek Orthodox Church a block ahead. There must have been two hundred people on their way inside. Cars littered the sides of the street and overflowed the parking lot. As I crept closer, I saw the traditional black limousine and hearse. I noticed the group standing nearest to the door of the church was comprised of very young people, and realized I'd read about the kid who died. He was 14... some kind of car accident.

The poor kid was barely fourteen.

Sadness supplanted my anger. I felt humbled.

My grip on the steering wheel loosened and my ire deflated.

I wondered what was worse—the inability to generate a biological child, or to birth one and watch it die before you? My situation was unfortunate. Their situation was tragic.

I pulled my truck over into a vacant parking lot and watched the crowd of mourners pour into the church. The volume of individuals created a backup outside. People embraced each other. Others cried.

I was medicated with a healthy dose of perspective.

I had thought my situation couldn't be worse. I was quickly reminded how wrong I was.

Cranking the truck back up, I signaled to leave the parking lot. My blinker caught my attention.

"Sorry about that business back there...you blink as loud as you want."

SPERM ROULETTE

As we dealt with our current stress and anticipated difficult decisions ahead, you can probably guess where we headed.

"You want some coffee or not?" asked Belinda, our waitress. She was curt, but she meant nothing by it—English wasn't her primary language, so we chalked up her occasional moments of impropriety to an issue of translation. She knew we were regulars and took care of us very well. As in most places in town, Kiersten didn't even have to open her mouth to order.

"You want your usual?" Belinda asked Kiersten.

"Yes please. Oh, could I get..."

"I'll get sugar-free syrup," Belinda said. Turning to me, she snarled, "And you? You're always different."

"Oatmeal, please," I said.

"You on a diet?" asked Belinda, goading me.

"You want me to keep coming back?" I asked.

"I'll get your coffee..."

"Okay, now tell me everything you talked about," Kiersten said.

"If you wanted to know everything, you really should have just come to the meeting."

I got the teacher stare. One bad step and I'd be in the corner.

"Okay, well—I'll tell you everything I remember."

I proceeded to tell her about DNA fragmentation, that it took place in South Dakota of all places, and that I had to go into that cursed room again and treat my body "like a circus" with a Sears catalog, to reference Ms. Costanza from *Seinfeld.*

"So what happens if the fragmentation test comes back positive—that there's a problem?" she asked.

"Believe it or not, I actually asked him that. If it comes back and my boys are shot then we can consider donor sperm. Or we just quit."

"And if it's fine?" she asked.

"Believe it or not, I actually asked that too."

"I'm very impressed," she said.

Gold star for me.

"If it comes back fine, then we know no more than we know now: that it's fine and we should be able to produce a pregnancy, but for some reason three rounds have come up empty," I explained.

"And then what?" she asked.

"Well, I think we decide which measures we want to take—we can do another round like last time, we can go to donors, etc."

"Or we can do nothing at all," she said.

"Or we can do nothing at all," I corroborated.

We both proceeded with our breakfast. I scooped up piles of oatmeal and let it slide off my spoon, largely because I was an adult and nobody could tell me not to play with my food anymore. This was acceptable behavior to me, not to mention therapeutic.

Kiersten, on the other hand, approached her breakfast with the attention of someone with obsessive-compulsive disorder. She devoured her slices of bacon entirely, then turned to her French toast. With calculating precision, she evenly spread the slices about her plate, applied butter, then poured the sugar-free syrup over them, and subsequently attacked them with her fork.

Poor French toast... never had a chance.

We both enjoyed a brief respite from reality.

I sat, staring out the window, tracking the paths of passers-by. Some were typical folk, others were mothers pushing babies in expensive baby-propelling apparatuses, while others appeared to be at or near homelessness. I wondered what made any of these people happy and what drove others to despair. Were they born into privilege or destitution? Did they have exceptionally well adjusted and nurturing parents or did nobody care for them? What made for a successful offspring versus those that led lives of frustration?

The mere act of people-watching had changed so dramatically in the span of 24 hours. We were facing the probability of never having a biological child, deciding about donor eggs and/or donor sperm based on the news that would arrive in a few days, or perhaps moving our adoption plans ahead of our biological plans. But the question of what makes a person content wouldn't leave me.

Am I content? What defines my happiness?

Soul searching over lukewarm oatmeal wasn't exactly my idea of a good time, but there I was nonetheless.

"You finished?" asked Belinda, making a face at my bowl of slop.

I looked down, made about the same face as she had, and agreed that I'd tortured those rolled oats enough. "Yeah, it's all yours."

THE PROFESSIONAL

My appointment was once again early in the morning. I didn't like to think about someone being in the "collection room" ahead of me. I knew people had been in there the day before and the day before that and so on, but at least giving the room 12 hours to 'air out' gave me some level of peace. You might recall how John Cage from *Ally McBeal* would use his toilet remote control to flush the can before he used it because he only liked to use a "fresh bowl." It was something like that.

This was my fourth trip to the dreaded collection room. I could spend the next couple of pages talking about how unfair all of this was and how miserable I was, but frankly, I was beginning to see the humor in the fact that when most people used their sick leave, they usually felt miserable. But me—the last four hours of sick leave I'd used were mostly spent looking at crummy pornography and diddling myself. That's not to say I didn't have coworkers who did the same, but at least I had an exceptionally good excuse.

By this time, my 'donating' had become almost routine.

I hustled down the stairs to the familiar office dungeon which resided in the basement of a medical facility. I flung

open the door and glanced briefly at the waiting room furniture, just to make sure I'd be safe during a flood. I
noticed my mother-in-law had calculated my arrival and
conveniently made an office coffee run.

Oh, thank God.

After all, this was almost as uncomfortable for her as it
was for me.

I hung a left and headed towards the collection room
featuring the couch which had no doubt contemplated
suicide dozens of times, if only the couch Gods had given
it some kind of dexterous appendage or perhaps opposable thumbs. I'd been in this office enough times by now
to know where they kept their treats — so I took a tempo-
rary detour into the break room and absconded with a
handful of grapes and an oatmeal cookie. *After all, I do
need my strength*, I thought.

I navigated the maze of mysterious little rooms with
haste, locating Ken's sperm hot plate and grabbing the
sack which displayed my name in bold black letters,
packed with care just like Mom's lunches in grade
school — except there was no tuna fish sandwich in this
bag. And I guess Mom never really used to encourage
the kind of behavior that my current brown paper bag
did.

Back to the room. There was the familiar sink. The
clock. The can. The crummy dirty rags, and my friend the
couch which dreamt of being reincarnated as a seagull
who would crap on Granderson's Audi each day. I pulled
the instructions out of the bag and glanced over them for
any relevant changes. I sat and wondered if they should
let me write new instructions.

This cup is for your stuff. Yes, it's a huge cup—don't worry, nobody can fill it. If you can, there's a movie industry that would like your services.

Please get all of the sample in the cup. If you miss the cup, you are having entirely too much fun in here and cleanup is YOUR responsibility.

There's no pressure for you to get this over with quickly, but understand that the office currently has a pool running on which patient will be the fastest in and out of the collection room. A meter started running when the door closed. Make us proud.

Prepare for the fact that our inspirational magazines may actually work contrary to their intended function. If you like big hair, heavy makeup, or if you thought the cast of A League of Their Own *was particularly attractive, proceed. If not, just use your imagination.*

Don't forget to write down the time you finish.

And be nice to the couch.

I sat on the edge of the couch and let out an extended, audible, sigh. The look on my face must have been similar Ben Stein's in *Ferris Bueller's Day Off* or perhaps Simon Cowell during a particularly uninspired vocal effort. Somewhere between disinterested and disgusted.

"For South Dakotans everywhere," I said as I unbuckled my drawers.

FROZEN GOODS

While I was perfecting my craft in the collection room, Kiersten perused the online profiles of sperm donors at California Cryobank, which was apparently the single largest repository of purchased spunk in the civilized world. I could only imagine the lineup of eager young men once word got out that you could get paid for jostling your John Thomas in lieu of wasting boxes of perfectly good Kleenex and explaining to mom that you got "bad allergies" in November. That she was shopping for someone else's sperm was a terrific vote of confidence for me, no less.

If you've never examined online sperm banks, you simply have to. You could slice and dice the donors any way you wanted—dark hair, light hair, brilliant, not-so-brilliant, tall, short, brawny, skinny, Hispanic, Caucasian, Filipino, you name it. You could probably concoct a freakishly tall albino and reincarnate the creepy killer guy from *Foul Play* with Goldie Hawn.

The idea was to choose someone so similar to the features of the male that there'd really be no question about whether or not the kid was biological as they grew up. Or,

I suppose, for any of the women out there that secretly couldn't stand the physical makeup of their partner, well—build your own Ken doll, if that's what you were looking for.

Scanning some of the donor profiles, I couldn't help but wonder if these guys had to look at Geena Davis naked while they left their deposits… although, for all I knew, they very well might have left them in the same decade when the magazines around my shop were actually published.

Kiersten excitedly emerged from our office. "Honey, I finally found one that I think could be a good match."

"Let me guess—profile just says 'fat, drunk, and stupid'?"

"How did you know?" she said. "No, really—this is a blond, blue-eyed, six-foot- tall Caucasian, with an advanced degree. It's really the only match I could find that I liked."

"Is that the only blond-haired, blue-eyed person on there?" I asked.

"Well, no—but there's a feature where the donor can actually write something about himself. It eliminated many of them. Some of them just seemed like idiots."

"I appreciate the fact that you didn't say those were dead ringers for me," I said.

"Well…" she said.

"Don't do it!"

"But really, what these guys had to say about themselves was just hilarious. You could tell some of them weren't the brightest," she said.

"So you didn't find many that seemed like good matches?"

"Actually, there were only a few who seemed to meet your physical profile, but there was just this one who had the strong education background along with having a decent writing sample," she said. "And it's weird—his writing actually *looked* like yours."

"Boy, it's too bad my boys are of questionable quality—they might actually be in high demand down at California Cryo! I'd have a second income!"

"Well, I know that you and he have something in common, though," she said.

"Besides the obvious?"

"Their profiles indicate whether or not they've ever created a pregnancy. He hadn't," she said.

"Well, how old is he, for crying out loud? He was probably 20 when he made the donation," I argued. "Am I half a man because I didn't impregnate a girlfriend from college?"

"No, not whether or not he has a child, but whether or not someone who's purchased his sperm has produced a baby," she said.

"Ah, I see. I imagine knowing that would be important, huh? I might have a pretty attractive donor profile too, but it might take some pretty eager eggs to work with my boys," I posited. "Who would have thought this would be so complex?"

Turning somewhat serious, Kiersten asked me, "Are you sure you're okay with all this donor business?"

"Sure, why not?" I said.

"Well, it's kinda crazy, isn't it?" she said.

"More crazy than harvesting your multiple eggs, injecting them with my sperm, forcing their implantation in you via a six inch catheter and then me force feeding hormones into your ass with a 22-gauge needle?"

"I guess that's a good point," she said.

"I have my moments."

But was I really okay with this donor business? With the verdict on my DNA a few days off, it was fairly easy to say I was open to any option. I wasn't about to close any door until a door was closed for me. The notion of sperm from someone else impregnating my wife didn't do much for me, not to mention the idea that someone else could use the same donor and our kid would have a dozen half-siblings running around out there. And really, can you imagine *paying* for spunk? I mean, how much stranger could this get?

I'd cross that bridge when I came to it.

EGGS, NEVER EASY

I walked in our back door, kicked my shoes off in the mudroom and entered the kitchen. Bella was there, looking hungry and sullen as always. Kiersten was on the phone...as always. Our after-work routine was often quite predictable: Kiersten beat me home and spent a good portion of the next half hour rehashing all the good gossip with her closest friends or making some kind of saucy evening plans while I slipped out of my monkey suit, deposited my work personality somewhere in the laundry bin and pulled on my baggy jeans and vintage shirt, welcoming my true persona back.

"That was my mother," she said. "You're not going to believe this."

"Do tell," I said.

"Well, she said that it's really important that we get back on the calendar quickly —apparently they have higher success rates for IVF rounds that are practically back-to-back," she reported.

"You're right! I don't believe that!" I said sarcastically.

"Will you let me finish?"

"Of course, please, proceed."

"Well," she said, gesturing wildly with both hands, "I figured we might as well get on the books whether we're using a donor or not, so they put us down in March."

She paused, leaning in at me, eyes opening wider, as if I was missing the obvious point. I hated that look; it was always something I would never, ever, think of.

"Um…I get the sense there's something wrong with March?" I said.

"*March*??" she repeated, giving me one more chance.

I looked down at my hands and started counting, one finger at a time, "March, April, May, June, July, August, September…"

She interrupted my progress. "Yeah, a December baby. In fact, a late December baby! Can you *even* believe it?"

I was laughing out loud before she could even finish her sentence.

"You're not seriously worried about that, are you? I mean, of all the damned things we can spend time being pissed off about—you're already upset about the kid's birthday for crying out loud?" I exclaimed.

"Well, it's just *perfect*!" she said.

"In fact, it is—it would be the perfect irony. It almost guarantees this will work," I hypothesized.

Kiersten had lost control of the due date, yet we were on the books. But the big question was whose parts would be making our kid.

*   *   *

Notwithstanding the prospect of an evening predestined to be filled with bizarre conversations of doomed December babies, modified fertility drug regimens, and donor sperm, we were both miserably underfed. Consequently, I took inventory of our cupboards.

We could fix peanut butter with popcorn, eat some freezer-burned sugar-free vanilla ice cream, split a jar of martini olives, or we could just go out to eat. The peanut butter probably had the most appeal nutritionally, but considering I usually used that jar to feed the dog scoops of peanut butter off of my index finger, dinner out seemed like the better and more sanitary choice.

We decided to go someplace within walking distance. It was always easier to rationalize the intake of copious calories if we burned a few getting there and back. The restaurant *du jour* was a southwestern cuisine eating spot—one of our local favorites. They had the greatest staff in town, and arguably the best food in town—although there were a few items on the menu to avoid. You see, this was a joint where you could actually order a few vegan meals, and although the menu descriptions sounded scrumptious, a couple of the dishes tasted like warmed cardboard with kale-eggplant paste. But as most regulars knew, there were some truly spectacular meals to be had there, not to mention great sangria The complimentary sopapilla was just sinful—combined with the accompanying honey-butter, it had to be about 400 calories a piece, but worth every fat-producing ounce.

We arrived at the restaurant, and the joint was wall-to-wall packed. We found our way to the waiting area where Kiersten ordered a glass of sangria and I fought the extremely loud voice in my head telling me to order a beer. I fantasized about the return of my DNA test which would very likely liberate me to infinite libations.

Could there be any possible way my boys' DNA didn't look like shredded wheat?

By the time we were seated, Kiersten was well on her way to her third sangria. I hypothesized that something had been on her mind and she was getting the conversation juices primed. We ordered our usual, the "Deluxe Blue Plate," a spicy little enchilada number whose flavor was simply unmatched. I broke down and ordered a ten-oz. beer— I sensed an impending heart-to-heart and I'd be damned if I didn't arm myself with a tiny buzz.

"So tell me again what we're doing if your DNA is bad?" she said.

I'm clairvoyant.

"Well, you and the Cali Cryobank have a date, I assume."

"And what if it's fine, your DNA," she asked, timing her question to the moment before she was about to sip her third glass of sangria, allowing herself enough time to get adequately acquainted with it before she was required to speak again.

"Well, then I guess we have some decisions to make. We could go for another round of IVF, we could just bag it and adopt, we could see if there's an egg issue…"

"I've been thinking a lot about those last two," she said. "It's entirely possible that my eggs are a bigger problem than your sperm."

"Well what would we do then? California CryoEggs?" I asked.

"Something that has occurred to me more than once is we could ask my sister to donate eggs. You know how much we look alike. I'm sure that our kid would still look exactly like our biological child," she said.

"Yeah, but isn't that just creepy? My sperm fertilizing your sister's eggs? I mean ... weird. Very, very weird," I said.

She sipped her sangria and eyed the basket of sopapilla.

I fiddled my hominy with my fork. *Hominy is such a fancy word for giant mushy corn nuts,* I thought to myself.

I broke the silence.

"I'm sorry, did we just talk about using your sister's eggs to produce our child?"

"I think we did," she said.

"Interesting," I said. "Is there anything that makes you think she'd actually want to do this?"

"I bet she would. I'm sure it's not something she'd be excited about, but I bet she would do it for us."

"Your sister's eggs," I said, verbalizing the idea just to make sure I understood it correctly. "So she'd have to go through the timed cycle thing, the ultrasounds, the hormone shots, the retrieval, the whole thing?"

"Yep," she said.

"Oh, I see—you just want to torture her!" I said, laughing long and loudly.

"Now, that's not true!"

"I know, I know..." I said. "But seriously, that's a hell of a lot to ask of your sister. And would you really want a kid that way? You know—every time you look at them, it occurs to you that they're really your sister's? Seems just... kind of... 'off,' doesn't it?"

"Any more 'off' than harvesting my eggs in a lab, injecting them with your sperm, forcing their implantation my uterus via a six inch catheter and then having you stab my ass with hormones?" she said.

Hmm…heard this argument somewhere before. It's strangely compelling.

"Well, you make an interesting point—but it still seems pretty weird to me."

"How are you guys doing over here?" asked our waitress, who bore a resemblance to the offspring of Kathy Bates and Captain Lou Albano, sans the rubber bands stapled on the face, of course.

Kiersten's expression became sheepish, almost guilt-ridden. "Can we get another order of sopapilla, please?"

"Another order of sopas, coming right up," said the waitress.

Kiersten gave the waitress a big grin and short little enthusiastic claps. "Oooh! I can't wait!"

The stuff was like heroin for a hypoglycemic like my wife. Sopas were the equivalent of sugar-free doughnuts and she was as addicted to them as Jim Carrey was to attention.

I sat and absorbed the moment. If the last year had taught me anything, it was to appreciate her smile. She was a tough chick, but genuine joy was hard to come by these days. I loved to see her happy—who cared if it was about food.

We left the issue of donors for another meal.

Many children, many cares;
no children, no felicity.

– Christian Nevell Bouvee

LOOKING FOR RESULTS-
ORIENTED SELF STARTER

Today was the day.

Today I'd find out if the very fiber that made up my microscopic reproductive cells was garbage. This was not your average ho-hum consultation about blood pressure and laying off the fudge with your family Doc. While I'm sure hundreds of thousands of people have received much more damning news from a physician in the last year, I was no less tense about the prospect of hearing that I had sperm DNA which appeared to be on acid and which would preclude me from ever producing a little Mr. or Miss Me.

The signs certainly pointed to bad or "fragmented" DNA. My wife was a few years my junior; she should certainly have good eggs. We'd achieved many fertilized embryos, but the fertilization has always had to come via ICSI, and none seemed to want to continue to grow after implantation. Frankly, I think a big part of Kiersten wanted it to come back positive for fragmentation—it would have given us a smoking gun, a clear reason, and we could then move on to what was supposed to be our second child — via adoption — and she would never need to endure another invasive round of IVF again.

When I had originally agreed to this fragmentation test, I assumed that I would be able to simply call in and get the results. I envisioned some kind of automated phone service via a 1-800 number, complete with the lifeless female voicemail lady:

Hello, you've reached the South Dakota sperm investigators.

If you have submitted a sample and you are calling for results, press one.

Thank you.

Please enter the last four digits of your social security number.

Thank you.

Please wait while we retrieve your record.

We have located the results of your sample test. Your sperm DNA is laughable.

Thank you for calling.

South Dakota sperm investigators wish you the very best. For South Dakota tourism information, press three ...

No such luck. I'd have to find out the results in person. What's worse, I'd have to find out the results back in that God-forsaken, almost-fainted-and-tossed-my-cookies room where I'd been twice before now. Granderson was going to give us the details of the test in person.

We unenthusiastically entered the office.

"My children!" exclaimed Kiersten's mother, both arms cast into the air with enthusiasm. "Michael Charles, look what I have for you!"

She reached into her purse, pulled out about three dollars in change and dumped it into my hands, smiling ear to ear. I wasn't sure why this gave her such intense joy, but who was I to complain—all in all, I'd really scored in the mother-in-law department. She babied me. And now I'd never ever get a ticket at metered parking.

"Michael Charles, come with me," she commanded. I was led into the break room where fresh baked cookies greeted me. She gestured dramatically toward then and proclaimed, "Linda made them just for you!"

"Did she really make them for me or did she make them for the office and you're just saying that she made them for me?" I inquired.

"Well, she doesn't know that she made them for you—but they really *are* for you," she said.

I raised my right eyebrow at her and grinned. "Hmm. Sounds pretty fishy."

Although her argument made little sense, her enthusiasm and unconditional love were undeniable.

I took two cookies.

She beamed.

We made our way back towards the front, where Kiersten was casually talking with Granderson and Linda.

"Is Michael Charles ready for the meeting yet?" he deadpanned.

"I'm armed with cookies and ready," I said.

We were led into the familiar room which had yet to deliver us any good news and sat on that damned uncomfortable ugly green and pink couch, which seemingly slugged an inch lower every time we sat on it.

"Well, I'm sure you guys are wondering about the results of the DNA fragmentation test," he said.

I shrugged my shoulders casually, almost as if to say, "DNA fragmentation test? What DNA fragmentation test?"

"Well, everything looks good," Doc said.

"What looks good—South Dakota? Lovely this time of year?" I said.

"There's no fragmentation. The DNA is sound. In fact, Ken did a workup of your sperm from this sample and there's apparently a great deal of improvement with your morphology and motility," he reported.

Uh...what room is this? Isn't this the kick-you-in-the-teeth, I've-only-got-shitty-news room?

I looked at Kiersten in amazement.

"Well, that's great!" she said in much the same way that she might if I came home and proclaimed, "Honey, look who I ran into—it's my old college roommate! He needs a place to stay and I told him he could sleep here for a few months. I'm going to the store for some malt liquor!"

"So everything is good? I'm really surprised," I said.

"Everything is good—in fact, things look even better," he said.

"So what's our problem?" I asked, cutting to the chase.

"Well, the fact that your DNA test came back fine doesn't necessarily mean there's still not a sperm issue," he said.

Then why the hell did we spend $500 to do it?

"There still could be a sperm issue, there could be an egg issue, it could be a little of both," Granderson said. "With this information, we basically eliminate one of the variables. We know more today than we did yesterday. With each round of in-vitro that you've gone through, we've learned a little bit more. So we're closer to knowing what it will take, but there are still unknowns."

He paused to adjust his glasses. I think he might have contemplated drawing a picture, but I believe it occurred to him that drawing a sperm donor wasn't terribly appropriate.

"So what would you suggest?" I asked.

"Well, your quickest route to a baby would be to use donors," he said.

"Donor what?" I asked.

"We'd start with donor sperm and if that didn't work well, then we would probably move to donor egg and then perhaps both," he said in a nonchalant way that suggested using other people to conceive your baby for you was as normal as changing a flat tire.

"Or you could do another blastocyst round like the last one," he added.

"Is doing another blast round a complete waste of time? Is there just no chance that it will work?" asked Kiersten.

"I don't think so at all. You two produced really great embryos last time, and we would probably change your drug regimen just a little bit this time based on what we learned. The embryos just don't seem to want to continue. It could have been just dumb luck for three rounds and it will work fine, or there might be a problem we just don't know about," he said.

"What would you guess our chances are if we did another blast round? What's the percentage?" I asked.

"Thirty," Doc answered.

"Thirty… like one in thirty?"

"Thirty percent," he clarified.

"I see. Much better, thank you."

Kiersten and I sat and stalled. It seemed the good doctor was out of information and he was looking to us to make some kind of decision.

We looked approvingly at each other, eyebrows raised, lips thoughtfully protruding, much the way a couple might if they were trying to decide between bed linens at the mall and the salesperson was hovering over them. The kind of look that said, "You make the decision, I have no idea." Or at least that's what that face meant for me.

"What would you do?" I asked Granderson.

"What would I do? You mean if I were you?"

"Yeah, sure—that."

"Well, I can't really say… but I can tell you that it is perfectly acceptable to go for another blastocyst round. I think that is a perfectly viable option," he said. "I also wouldn't blame you if you wanted to go straight to donor. I think either is a good option for you right now."

"Good relatively speaking, of course," I said.

He looked at me, confused.

"Well, frankly, both options pretty much suck in my opinion," I said, grinning.

"Oh, I get it—yeah, I can see that," he said, although I still wasn't sure he'd understood my little joke.

"I suppose we'll have to think about what we want to do next," said Kiersten, clearly having had enough of my random banter with Granderson. "Thank you very much for everything—we'll talk it over and get back to you."

We all shook hands. After exchanging some niceties with the mother-in-law and the rest of the staff, we exited the office and both let out a heavy sigh.

"Feel like a drink?" I asked.

"You read my mind," she said.

LAST CALL

After our informational meeting with Granderson about my now-nearly-normal sperm, we took a day to decompress. Under normal circumstances, we would deal with stress by running up a credit card shopping at a discount clothing retailer or by slowly consuming a bottle of Tanqueray (you can puzzle out which of us is attached to which of the activities described). But unfortunately, we had neither the money to shop nor the quality of sperm to drink.

It had been an excruciatingly stressful year filled with decisions that neither of us thought we would ever need to make. As a married pair, I figured we'd be faced with some interesting decisions, of course.

30-year fixed versus seven-year variable ARM mortgage? Yeah.

Antique light fixtures versus reproduction? Absolutely.

Wagon for utility versus sedan for sport? For sure.

In-vitro fertilization, intra-cytoplasmic sperm injection, DNA fragmentation, and donor goods to reproduce? Not particularly.

We gave ourselves 24 hours to merely live without having to dialogue about donors, medicines, finances, or anything besides just reacting to what life put in front of us for a day. It was decidedly liberating. Despite the fact that we both had the cloud of indecision and the unknown oppressively looming over our heads, our daily routines were reduced to the predictable tango that they were. It was a much-needed respite from the complexity of our reality into parsimonious schedule-keeping.

I recall a moment in my life when I once had a complete stranger help me appreciate simplicity, though I didn't realize it until much later. In college, I tore my Achilles tendon. At the hospital, noticing my struggle to maneuver my crutches post-surgery, an elderly gentleman told me what was supposedly a Chinese proverb. "When you walk, *know* that you are walking," he said.

Who are you, Caine from 'Kung Fu'?

At the time, I thought he was either just insane or he made a habit of arbitrarily reciting his fortune-cookie ticket to strangers on crutches. Who knows, perhaps he actually was insane. But for some reason, his comment stuck with me for years: Don't take for granted the simple, the expected, the assumed. Appreciate the beauty of the ordinary.

I thought of him again today.

If life were only this uncomplicated. If only our life played out like we scripted it.

Our salvation throughout the trials of the past year was our unity in decision making. For better or for worse, our choices with regard to this pursuit, this kid quest, were made without a hint of dissent. We were ironclad in our unity. On the proverbial same page.

The subsequent day, a hole appeared in the dam.

"So now that we know you don't have any fragmented DNA, how are you feeling about donors?" Kiersten asked.

"I'm not into it. I'm not into it at all," I said. "Sorry, I know how much you love that California Franken-Bank, but I just can't get behind the idea."

"Yeah, I tend to agree," she said.

"What about the whole idea of your sister's eggs?" I asked.

"I don't think it makes any sense. I really feel like we're at a point where maybe this is a sign—maybe we're just not supposed to have a biological child right now."

"Yeah, it's certainly beginning to feel that way," I said.

"We're already planning on adopting, it was just a matter of when," she said. "Why would we want to use donors when we know there's a baby out there right now that we could adopt?"

I sensed a mutual understanding coming. We'd just pursue a fourth round aggressively and see if it produced a healthy pregnancy. If not, perhaps we'd be lucky enough to have several fertilized embryos to freeze and we'd have one or two subsequent shots left. If we were fed the same diet of ugly news, then we'd assume that our biological child was, indeed, destined to be the Antichrist, and happily move on to our adoption plans a year or two early. The plan was flawless. Well, as flawless as a plan could be for two people hopelessly pursuing parenthood against seemingly gigantic odds. There was no possible way we could emerge from the fourth round without some kind of positive outcome. A baby awaited us.

"I'll tell you this much, though—I'm *not* going through that again," she said.

"You won't have to. This will be our last shot."

"No, I'm not doing another round of IVF," she said definitively. "I've thought about it and I'm just not going to put myself through that again."

"Really," I said, in a way that was more a statement than a question.

Sandbags. I need lots of sandbags.

"I think we should start the paperwork for adoption," she said. "Now."

"Really," I said again, realizing that we were very clearly standing on two separate pages. In between these pages lived doubt, disappointment, weeks of intramuscular shots, but also possibility and hope. There was a chasm between our preferences and I was attempting to adjudicate between my interest in what I thought our best option was and what my wife would need to go through to do it my way. Somewhere in there existed her happiness—and I was getting damned tired of the choose-your-own-adventure pathway towards trying to find it. Would she always wonder "what if" should we go her route? Would we be back in the chili-dog room five years from now because she wanted to give it one last shot? Should we see the process through with this last round?

"You think we've adequately seen this process through?" I asked.

"Michael, we've done three rounds and had absolutely no success—we're young enough that we should have had much better results," she said.

But I'm looking so much thinner! I'll be 160 lbs after another round!

"Well, do I have to remind you that we *were* pregnant once?" I said.

She paused, staring deeply across the room towards our 30s-era German grandfather clock, tracking our conversation methodically with each audible tick and tock.

"No," she said flatly.

I felt like shit dredging up old pain.

"I just feel like our first round was successful, but didn't continue for some reason; the second round was shot because you were sick; and the third round was shot because of your fever," I said. "It just feels like we're due for a clean round—we've learned more about me, about us, they'll try a new and improved drug regimen this time, and we owe it to ourselves to complete this experience."

She looked at me, unconvinced.

Kiersten was tired. Weary from the shots, the drugs, the invasive procedures. But more than anything, tired of the disappointment. It was all over her face and I could see it plainly. And I certainly couldn't blame her. But I couldn't escape the feeling that she would always want to know what the result of the fourth round would have been. I wanted resolution—I could handle another let-down if it un-muddied the water.

"I've had it with the waiting, Michael," she said with slow, clear articulation so as not to be misunderstood. "You know how badly I've always wanted to adopt and I just think we should start that right now instead of continuing with something that clearly doesn't give us a great chance."

"You know I want that too, but do you think you'll be okay with walking away right now?" I asked.

"Yes," she said definitively.

"Okay then."

"But I can tell that you won't be," she said.

"What does it matter what I think?" I asked.

"You're a part of this too, you know."

"Yeah, but I win either way— ultimately we get something we both want," I said. "The way I see it, we're just arguing about fiddling with the order. I'm more worried about your state—whether you're truly ready to move on."

"Why would you say that I'm not?"

"I don't know—I'm not a female," I said. "I don't know about the impulse to carry a child. I don't have those parts. I'm not sure what you're feeling. I guess I'm just assuming that it's something that is important to most women—the experience, the announcements, the showers, the birth, the whole thing."

She sat and stared at the rug. Not in a dejected kind of way, but more in a manner that suggested she was pissed off that I'd actually brought up a decent argument. My rationale seemed to strike a nerve.

"Well, I'll do it for you, because that's obviously what you want," she said.

"Oh, no, no, no… that is most definitely *not* what I want," I retorted. "I want what you want. I want what *we* want. I absolutely don't want you doing something for me."

"But if you think that…"

"No, seriously—you're not doing anything for me," I said. "Period."

I got up to get a drink. Enough of this crazy talk. I could have eight ounces of wine tonight and, by God, it was going down in the next five minutes.

While she waited for me to cork the bottle and pour the wine, Kiersten placed a disc in the DVD player—some romantic comedy that I'd ordered from Blockbuster.com because I thought it would make Kiersten smile despite the fact that I'd wince all the way through, like watching a 5-year-old play with a slingshot.

We sat and watched the movie without a word about in-vitro fertilization. I think it was Mark Ruffalo and Reese Witherspoon in some odious mess of a movie, but I could tell Kiersten was enjoying it so I spared her my typical "oh, you've got to be kidding me" and "who the hell writes this stuff" comments which I spout off when movies bring me near physical sickness.

The reprieve was appreciated on both of our parts. Distraction by television. We'd hit the point where a married couple knew that if either of us said anything, it would probably be enough to put our relationship in jeopardy. Well, perhaps not in jeopardy, but it would at least be the kind of conversation you work hard to avoid, the kind of talk that makes your overdramatic 8-year-old daughter run into the room in her pink pajamas and scream, tears streaming down her face, "I HATE IT WHEN YOU FIGHT! DON'T GET A DIVORCE, PLEASE!!!" Although there was no 8-year-old in sight, I wanted to avoid it nonetheless.

The movie ended. I was near hysterical from the stupidity of it, but I calmly placed the DVD back in the sleeve, wondering how the hell I could get involved in an industry that burns human waste on a shiny disc and calls it entertainment. Meanwhile, Kiersten gathered up our popcorn bowls and delicately placed them in the dishwasher.

I swear to God we both patted the trunk of the giant elephant which was standing in our den as we made our way to bed. But we didn't dare speak of it.

Familiarity breeds contempt... and children.

– Mark Twain, *Notebooks* 1935

CLOSURE

Anything related to in-vitro fertilization was avoided until I got home from work the next day. But when I did, I made a surprising discovery. Kiersten was suddenly on board for the fourth round.

"I was on the phone for forever ordering my medication," she said casually.

"Medication…" I said, inquisitive, as if I thought I knew what she was talking about, but just wanted to hear her say it.

"The Repronex and Follistim, the usual," she nonchalantly reported.

"Uh…" I staggered.

"You wouldn't believe how long it took," she said.

"Wha…umm…why…why are we ordering the medication?"

"Our cycle is coming up fast — we need the medication right away," she said. "We can't wait."

"Yeah, but we didn't necessarily decide that we were going to go through with this round, did we?"

"I know this is what you want, though," she said. "I talked to my mom and…"

"You talked to your mom and she convinced you that you needed to do this for me," I interjected with a callousness that surprised even me.

Kiersten didn't immediately respond.

"Am I right?" I persisted.

As if watching mercury move from shade to sun on a July day in Albuquerque, she could see my ire escalate.

"No, I think we should do this round too," she said, as if she had rehearsed saying it on the way home. It was the same tone in which appeasing wives say, "No, I think going to the ballgame is a good idea," or "Yes, I think that neon beer sign looks great on the wall," and "No, really—I think anal sex feels good."

"I'm sorry, but to hell with that," I said. "Seriously, I see right through this. You're doing this for me. I appreciate it, but if you're not 100 percent behind this, there's no damned way I want any part of it."

I wasn't angry, just supremely frustrated. I'm sure if I were to psychoanalyze our conversation, I'd say my word choice lacked empathy, but there was absolutely zero chance that I'd let her go through another round of IVF just because of my desire to challenge fate. I was convinced that unless she was fully sold on the idea—unless she thought there was a very good probability that it would work—it was entirely futile to bother. It would be a waste of our time and the doc's time, not to mention a tremendous waste of money, of which we were rapidly running out.

"I'm okay with it, though," she said. "We can do this round and then…"

"You can go through the motions of this round, that's what you'll do," I said. "There's no fucking way this works unless you actually think it will work."

"I thought it would work every other time and that didn't do me much good," she argued.

"So you'll just walk into this one, lower your expectations, go through the routine assuming it won't work, just for my sake?" I asked. "You really want me to pump you full of hormones just to satisfy what I think you need?"

"You need closure to this," she said.

"Is that what this is about?" I asked. "Because I don't want fucking closure. Closure suggests an ending. I want a beginning. I want you to be happy so we can move on."

"Well, *I'm trying* to move on," she said.

"And I just don't think you'll be truly happy unless we see this through."

"That's fine, so let's see it through."

"But you don't believe in it!" I said. "What's the point?"

We went around and around like this for another hour and made little progress. She was resigned to doing another round of IVF and I urged her to admit that she needed to do it because our last two rounds just weren't fair to us. We eventually left the topic alone. She cozied up to a book and I spent the next hour scanning baseball box scores online.

I began to understand why it appeared that I needed this fourth round for "closure," despite the fact that I hated that irritating word. But the fact was, I felt this lingering sense of unfinished business. It was as if I had been called out on strikes in each of my three at-bats and I disagreed with every single call, and just wanted an opportunity to hit a home run in my last plate appearance. It wasn't that I so desperately wanted a biological child—I had a strong calling to adopt. It was that I didn't feel like we had put proper punctuation on the sentence—that we were leaving this chapter in our reproductive novel terribly incomplete. And I felt like I knew Kiersten would feel it too. When she did, we'd be back in the middle of the same mess—and I wanted to avoid that like I avoided my dog when someone fed her spicy meatballs.

Is that needing closure? Maybe. But I wouldn't let her sacrifice her body and become a pincushion for hormone injections and a willing escort for an eager ultrasound stick for my "lingering sense." No way.

I decided to absorb myself in my most recent marginally interesting book. I turned the lamp on and saw the dusty forgotten diaper bag in the corner. Just perfect. After showering that bag and Ms. Petunia Picklebottom with obscenities, I grumbled, "I hope you're freaking comfortable there."

*   *   *

The following morning, I called the clinic and asked Kiersten's mother to put a hold on the medication. I could tell that she wasn't thrilled with the idea. She thought we should do this fourth round too. But I explained that my intentions were to talk it through with Kiersten first—that we hadn't made a decision together yet.

She acquiesced and called Kiersten's doctor's office. You might be wondering how her mother could make changes to Kiersten's personal medical decisions—but recall that her mother was also the representative for the in-vitro clinic and this was a common occurrence for her in her job. However, she accidentally cancelled the whole order.

About an hour later, I got a call from Kiersten.

"Do you know anything about my medication getting cancelled?" she asked. Her tenor was unmistakable—she was clearly pissed.

I knew this tone. It had a caught-red-handed quality. It was the same tone my Dad used when I was 3 years old as he asked, "Michael, did you write on this wall?!" I just so happened to be sitting with my crayons adjacent to the very spot at which he was pointing. It was that rhetorical question tone, except it actually necessitated an answer.

I sighed heavily.

"I don't know anything about it getting cancelled, but I did ask your mother to put a hold on it," I said.

"I spent my entire planning period on the phone ordering that yesterday!" she said.

For you non-teachers out there, wasting a planning period is like taking a week's vacation and spending it cleaning small-mouthed bass. It was an unconscionable abuse of free time.

"Well, I'm sorry about that," I said rather dispassionately. "But I just think that we need to arrive at a mutual decision about this before we spend that kind of money on medication we might not need. Don't you?"

She was silent. I could sense how frustrated she was with me. I could almost feel my phone receiver boiling in my ear.

I couldn't think of anything to say. A wedge had been driven between us and now not only were we dealing with infertility and this difficult decision, we were trying to deal with a rift in our ability to communicate.

I began to wonder if there was research about the marital status of couples who have gone through infertility treatment. The statistician in my head started to regress a myriad of independent variables against a dichotomous dependent variable of marital status, divorced or married.

Nerd alert.

I needed to collect my composure. Just get her home, we would talk this through and we'd move on. We couldn't let this get out of control. I wondered to myself, WWDPD (what would Dr. Phil do)?

First of all, I'd grandstand. Then I'd do something really smart and sensitive.

"Hon, I'm sure we can get the medicine ordered again," I said. "Can you just wait until we have a chance to talk about it tonight and then we can proceed? We'll deal with everything tonight, okay?"

"Okay," she said, dissatisfied, but more understanding now than two minutes ago.

I am shaving my head, growing a moustache, adopting a southern accent, and calling Oprah as soon as I get home.

*　　*　　*

That evening, we both chose seats on opposite ends of my singular masterpiece of interior design. When we moved in, our den was a 13-by-13 box featuring a 1980s ceiling fan and mint green walls; but with 100-plus-year-old six-panel pocket doors made of vertical grain fir, along with baseboard and window trim to match, the room had great potential. By the time we were done with it, it was fit for a vampire. The walls were painted a red so dark that the color fluctuated among various shades of blood all day long. Brown leather furniture, dramatic extra-large tropical foliage, and an over-sized traditional Chinese wedding cabinet were outdone only by the eight-foot gold chenille drapes and the antique Victorian chandelier with hand-painted exposed red bulbs (yes, I had been told I'm just the "right amount of gay," which I took as a compliment). Nothing bad could happen in this room, it was simply too damned cool.

It was therefore no surprise that our conversation that night was truly open. We allowed all of our suspicions, anxieties, and anger to spill out onto the floor in front of us for inspection. In the process, we discovered we weren't so far apart in our preferences.

"I just want to adopt," she said. "Like right now. I already have the adoption agencies narrowed down to two. Why waste time on another in-vitro round?"

"I want to adopt too, Kiersten," I said. "You know that I do. But I just know how Type A you are, and that you never fail at *anything*, and I'm worried that you're going to feel like we didn't do everything we could with in-vitro. I'm worried that we'll be back in that clinic years from now because you'll have a drive to do so."

"Well, I won't," she said without hesitation.

"I think you're wrong."

"Why do you want to keep doing this so badly?" she asked.

"I don't want to keep doing this, I just want to make sure your brain registers the fact that we've given in-vitro a fair shake and that we won't need to revisit this madness unless we really choose to, as opposed to *having to*," I said.

"So if we did a fourth round and it didn't work, you wouldn't want to keep doing this?" she asked.

"God no," I said. "Is that what you think?"

"That's the way it feels."

"Well, if we did a fourth round—a *clean* fourth round, no surprises—and it didn't work, I'd have absolutely no inclination to do another one unless you actually do," I said.

"Well I kind of think we should do another round too, I just want to make sure that you're not going to be one of those people that has to do IVF a dozen times or until it works," she said.

It was one of those moments as a couple dealing with problems when you almost couldn't avoid asking, *"WHY IN THE NAME OF GOD DIDN'T YOU SAY THAT A LONG FUCKING TIME AGO???"* but you were just so happy that you'd made a breakthrough that you leave it alone.

"Now, why would I want you to birth the Antichrist?"

"Real funny."

"So that's what this is all about—you think I'm going to *make you* do this forever?" I asked.

"Well…"

"Like we could even afford what we've gone through already!" I said.

"No kidding."

The cloud is lifting.

"Wine?" I asked.

"Mmmm…" she hummed.

That meant yes.

I poured us each a glass of wine, mine of course not more than eight ounces. We silently sat and sipped, allowing the air to clear. There was a palpable sense that we were going to get through this after all.

"I'm just…" she started to say.

Oh, no…

"…so tired of the waiting," she said.

Hmm…could have been worse. Waiting for what?

"If this fourth round doesn't work, we just lost another six weeks towards the adoption process. We're already looking at a year-plus if we go through China."

"Well, what stops us from doing both?" I asked.

"We would risk the $500 agency application fee," she said.

"In the scope of how much we've paid, the application fee is a minor nuisance," I said. "If you want to start the adoption process now, I'm all for it."

"*Really?*" Kiersten asked, eagerly.

"Yeah, let's do it," I said. "If this round is a dud, then we've lost nothing but money—and we really can't even lose what we don't have—so we really lose nothing. Am I wrong, or did we just figure out a win-win situation? It works, we move forward and adopt later, as per our original plan. It doesn't work, screw the plan, we're already knee deep in adoption paperwork."

"What happens if we wind up with a bunch of frozen fertilized embryos left over?" Kiersten asked.

"Then we just reverse the plan," I said. "We adopt, then go back to our biological batch of popsicles in a few years. What's the rush? They won't know the difference!"

Kiersten sat up, gears clearly turning in her skull. She was staring into nothingness with that daydreaming kind of look. It was the same look I got when someone suggested that we could do next year's fantasy baseball draft in Las Vegas.

"Well…I suppose I'll start the adoption application tonight," she said. "Are you sure?"

"I am. Are you?"

"Yeah."

She was smiling, clearly excited.

Was it the wine? Who knows. But we had a plan, and it felt great.

What's more, I had an eight-ounce wine buzz. Oh, sweet lack of tolerance.

*Nothing is so awesomely unfamiliar
as the familiar that reveals itself
at the end of the day.*

- Cynthia Ozick

DOUBLING DOWN

After three rounds of in-vitro fertilization—*three ago-nizing failures*—and all the emotional tumult associated with each letdown, you'd have thought we'd be viewing life through screw-the-world-and-your-baby tinted glasses. But a strange thing happened when we made a definitive decision about our future and children. When we decided this was our last round of in-vitro, and we were going to pursue adoption simultaneously, unbeknownst to us, we had purchased something entirely invaluable to our emotional health.

We discovered hope.

Suddenly, a conversation which felt like it threatened our entire relationship had produced an unanticipated silver lining.

We couldn't lose.

It was a baby ringer.

A can't-miss.

On the one hand, we had a possible-yet-increasingly-unlikely baby via in-vitro, and on the other we had the Sure Thing. What was supposed to be Baby #2 according to "the plan" was now our candidate to arrive as Baby #1.

That is, of course, unless God Himself looked down and took some kind of twisted pleasure in reverting us back to "the plan," and watching us lose the $500 adoption application fee. If so, it would further solidify my notion that God has a distinct appreciation of irony.

Embracing our situation, we pursued our fourth round with workmanlike diligence. Kiersten iced her upper thigh as I mixed sodium chloride with Repronex, measured out the Follistim, mixed that in, drew out 1 cc of fluid, removed the mixing needle, screwed on the 22-gauge needle, alcohol-swabbed the shot destination, readied the band-aid, injected, plunged, removed, cotton-balled and band-aided her, and then corked some wine and consumed.

We did this day after day, free of the typical stress and concern surrounding our doubts about the process working. We did it with complete blind faith that whatever happened … happened. We had surrendered control, and it felt fantastic. Liberating. Redeeming.

And then, per our agreement, we pursued the adoption process.

The paperwork for adopting a child was extraordinary. Extraordinary, as in paperwork two feet high. I'm convinced that if the powers that be made everyone who wanted to have a biological child go through this process, we'd be about five billion people shy of where we're at right now. Condom companies would rule the land like big oil does today. There would be a worldwide pull-out campaign by international political leaders for fear that if conception went unmitigated, the global economy would grind to a halt as workers everywhere took time off to finish their paperwork.

And yet, the lengths to which people were required to go in order to bring a child from another country to their own made sense to me. Considering all of the sick bastards in the world, I'd expect the equivalent of a personality full body cavity search in order to adopt. Turned out, the process to adopt from China was close. So I assumed the position.

First there was the application to the agency, which was roughly eight pages long. They wanted the usual— name, address, social security number, date of birth, how to contact us, etc. But it got a little interesting from there. Previous marriage history, arrest history, height and weight, medical history (including alcohol usage—good thing they weren't looking for an estimate on total lifetime alcohol intake). The sum of your life insurance, your health care provider, an extensive account of assets and liabilities—and if that wasn't sobering enough, they wanted you to include a statement about how exactly you planned to pay for this adoption. I didn't have the guts to tell them that I was planning on paying for it by donating sperm.

If you were accepted by the agency, good for you. Your check was summarily cashed and now the work really began.

First, you needed to find yourself a social worker. Ours necessitated an eighteen-page autobiography. With responses, it reached near 30 pages—60 for our combined responses. You think I'm kidding, and while I wish I were, this is agonizingly true. This was one of the most painful exercises I'd ever endured due to the fact that I had a sarcastic one-liner response for the majority of the questions. And yet I knew I couldn't use them because Kiersten would, no doubt, divorce me when she read it. Here's a very small sample of the questions and my *desired* replies for your enjoyment:

What was your father's role in your family?

To make money, drink scotch, and watch Knight Rider with me.

What was your mother's role?

Wonder what alien abducted my sister and replaced her with this monster. And buy scotch for Dad.

Describe your parents' marriage.

Praying to God that the aliens return my sister.

How did they show affection to each other?

Does slapping an ass count?

How did your parents comfort you?

They put a TV in my room.

How did they criticize you?

They threatened to take away the TV.

How did they praise you?

Cable.

How did your parents solve problems?

Rock, Paper, Scissors.

What difficulties did you encounter as a child?

The legal drinking age seemed excessive.

Where did you live growing up? Describe your life.

Suburban hell.

Were there other significant people in your life as a child?

Yes, Mr. Drummond from Different Strokes *and Potsie from* Happy Days.

What did you like about school?

Great weed.

What didn't you like about school?

Classes seemed to interfere with smoking weed.

Describe your current and past circle of friends.

Tanqueray, Makers Mark, Jim Beam, Jack Daniels...do I need to name them all?

At what age did you begin to date? Describe your early dating experiences.

Fifteen. I recall sweating a lot and wondering when I'd get to go home and watch The A-Team.

At what age did you consider yourself an adult?

I'll let you know.

How do you think others would describe your personality?

He's a sarcastic prick, but fun to drink with.

How do you handle job-related stress?

I am rubber, you are glue, what you say bounces off of me and sticks to you.

How frequently do you drink alcoholic beverages?

Mom, is that you?

Are you infertile? Please describe attempts to solve infertility issues.

Screw you.

How have you dealt with infertility?

Hating the fertile.

What's the biggest problem you've had to face as an adult?

Filling out this questionnaire.

What attracted you to your spouse?

Fine, fine boo-tay!

How are your family finances handled?

When creditors call, speak Spanish.

How do you divide household tasks?

When Kiersten trips over my shoes, she puts one away and throws the other one at me.

Please describe any differences in opinion you experience in your marriage.

Haven't yet sold her on the concept of daily fellatio.

What do you do together?

Recently, I've taken to giving her intramuscular shots and sometimes I masturbate in isolated office rooms when she's down the hallway. Is that weird?

What religion are you? Are you active in this faith? How often do you go to church?

Seriously, Mom? Is that you?

How would you manage as a single parent?

I'd try to ignore being single while I was managing but once the ballgame was over I'd see about getting a date.

How will adoption affect your biological children?

Seriously, SCREW YOU.

What are your future goals?

To get through this questionnaire and have a martini.

Truth be told, this is just a fraction of the questions. I'll spare you the remainder.

Each question was answered as sincerely as possible, of course, because we needed to appease the gatekeeper—our social worker. But the paperwork certainly didn't stop there. We also needed to complete a criminal background history, fill out net-worth reports, disclose full bank statements, not to mention have a thorough personal health report verified by a physician.

To add in the truly bizarre, we were also required to have three friends actually write us letters of recommendation, detailing their perceptions of our abilities to be good parents. We chose three of our closest friends, who no doubt had volumes to say about the maternal instincts of my wife, but I'm sure they struggled to figure out how golf and gin helped me become a better father.

Lastly, we were required to send along eight pictures of us with family and friends in social settings, ostensibly to prove to the Chinese that we were not both anthropophobiacs (fearful of other people). What's more, we were informed that many Chinese find it barbaric to have a dog as a pet, so we couldn't even send pictures of us with our drooling beast, Bella. Considering every photo we had in recent history featured a bottle of some kind of alcoholic beverage in my hand, we were in line for dozens of pictures with anyone who walked in our house.

Hi, good to see you. Can I take your coat? Okay, say cheese!

As we progressed through the paperwork, I soon discovered that I should have befriended a public notary long ago. If you have a notary in your back pocket during the adoption process, you will save an incalculable amount of money, not to mention a tremendous chunk of time. Because not only is there a heap of paperwork to fill out, but every last sheet of paper needs to be notarized, an approval imprint from some certified impartial party.

I'm not sure what's involved in becoming a notary, but based on our experience, the required qualifications must be right up there with "must have central nervous system." Some of the notaries we encountered throughout this process honestly did not look confident enough in their abilities to use Velcro.

Knowing that you were sending the material to the most meticulous and demanding of countries, you wanted a notary who slams that stamp down on the pages with confidence and conviction. Unfortunately, I saw two notaries actually shrug their shoulders as they applied their imprint to our paperwork, as if to say, "Hmm, I'm not sure if this will work, but let's give it a shot."

Amidst our paperwork challenge, we continued to live our double lives, literally carrying out two potential parental endeavors. Throughout our red tape and nincompoop-notary ordeal, we also had the typical ultrasounds and consultations at the in-vitro lab. As far as the erector-set science baby was concerned, things apparently couldn't look any better. Kiersten was producing world-class eggs, according to Doc—and there were upwards of a dozen in there. The staff delighted in the size and quality of her eggs, telling us how well things were going as we scheduled the retrieval for the following week.

We viewed it all with veteran suspicion, guarding against getting our hopes up once again. But our newfound nonchalance and stress-free attitude tended to drape this fourth round with a sense of possibility that neither of us could deny. This round felt different to both of us. The tower of stress and anxiety had toppled, and in its place was eager anticipation to move on with our life. That, coupled with the fact that the due date for this little sci-fi shaver was in the dreaded month of December (the 24th, no less) seemed to cement the likelihood that this could, indeed, work.

The week leading up to the retrieval was a blur of adoption paperwork, hormone injections, and photo opportunities with acquaintances. It was hard to keep straight what activity was tied to which parental effort. We also spent a good deal of time talking about our future little girl, our adopted daughter-to-be. Regardless of how the in-vitro turned out, we knew we would adopt at some stage in our life—either now or later.

We had decided on adopting from China. We were compelled to give a chance to a little girl who was abandoned for social and political reasons. We spent more time looking over adoption blogs and resources, talking about the places we would love to visit while we were there, and Kiersten was already hatching plans for what color to paint her room, what kind of baby furniture to get, and what would adorn the walls. We were both getting genuinely excited about adoption, already falling in love with this little girl whom we had never met, whose country we had never even visited.

But these plans would need to wait just a bit longer, as our retrieval date was upon us. I took another day off of work, Kiersten donned her familiar pajamas and we left for our last in-vitro attempt.

*   *   *

Driving to the appointment, my brain was engaged in a battle of superstition versus rationality.

Relax and just let this be what it is… the last time we will ever have to do in-vitro. Don't get worked up. Don't get too hopeful.

And yet everywhere along the way, I was looking for signs.

I hit a string of green lights and wondered if it was symbolic of something.

God, that's stupid—knock it off. How would you really feel if the cosmos communicated to you through traffic lights?

The sedan to my left had an empty baby car seat in it. Did that mean this definitely won't work? Or did it mean there was a baby on the way to fill the void?

It means that kid was just dropped off at daycare, you idiot.

We pulled into the parking lot. Each space was numbered. Despite the fact that there was a space near the door, I pulled forward into space #7.

"What was wrong with that one?" Kiersten asked, gesturing towards the convenient spot 100 feet closer.

"Number 13," I said.

"You're hilarious."

Or I'm a moron.

Being unable to procreate was like being an amputee, but nobody ever told you what you were missing. It was an assumed skill, an implicit right—and it was difficult to accept the reality of our circumstances. I'd heard people who have lost limbs talk about how they still feel an itch on their ghost extremity. I identified with that, but I couldn't tell you where the itch was coming from. It was a splinter I couldn't reach. I'd never had kids, but I swear I knew them. I simply couldn't figure out a way to get them here.

We walked into the clinic, and the familiar looks penetrated us. Like we were missing something. Like they felt badly for us.

Yet this round of in-vitro was the "super-cycle," as Granderson would put it. Everything was looking as good as it possibly could. Ken shared his enthusiasm, tossing a couple of comments my way about the newfound strength of my boys. "I have no doubt this'll work," he said. "Whatever you've been doing, your sperm is first-rate — these are going to fertilize in a jiffy."

In the chili-dog room, I met the anesthesiologist.

"She's got a tendency to reveal lots of classified information in here, so I hope you are sworn to strict confidentiality," I said.

"It all stays in this room, I promise," he said.

Kiersten didn't look apprehensive, as she had twice before in this very position. She was ready to get this over with, whatever the outcome. There was a baby at the end of this tunnel, and when she woke up from the blackout into which this over-educated man with the narcotics would put her, it would be the last time anyone physically removed her eggs. It was akin to never having to have your prostate checked again, multiplied by about one thousand. Her calm instilled confidence in me.

Granderson entered and pulled down the screen, revealing Ken in his army-green scrubs. There was the sound again.

Click-whiirrr…

Ken waved to us, enthusiastic as always. Watching him in his scrubs, I suddenly imagined a series of kids' books similar to "Where's Waldo," but in this book, you'd try to find Ken in a maze of hospital green, nurses, patients, and mysterious medical equipment. Partially hidden in some unlikely spot would be Ken in his green scrubs, smiling and waving.

"You guys ready to have a baby?" asked Granderson.

As opposed to the last three times we were here?? Oh, yeah — we were just faking.

"Ready," I said, having already prepared my straight-man face. No need for any more sarcasm in the chili-dog room, as this was weird enough to begin with.

I saw the anesthesiologist start the IV and knew Kiersten's consciousness was due to rapidly exit about as fast as Paris Hilton at a mathematics conference. In a ritual that felt like standard procedure by now, I kissed her on the forehead and told her I loved her and that everything would be okay. I read that sequence somewhere in a book once, perhaps *Marriage for Dummies*, or maybe it was *What to Expect When You're Expecting to Expect and it's Not Fucking Working*.

Or not.

Secretly, I wondered what I had done wrong since I wasn't invited back into 'Ken's House of Embryos' this time, but maybe they'd deemed my presence as bad luck and they didn't want me to jinx the remainder of the hundreds of fertilized embryos back there. Regardless, I summarily left the chili-dog room to suffer through the next half hour wondering how things were going as they dredged my wife's uterus. In previous in-vitro rounds, I would find myself in the lobby reading one of Granderson's magazines about golf, trying to find my "inner Tiger." Woods, that is.

But this was our third egg retrieval, and it seemed like the staff were becoming increasingly comfortable with our presence around the office. So instead of sifting through a dozen baby magazines looking for anything related to sports while I sat on my floatation-device loveseat, I was invited to the break room for homemade cookies, coffee, the daily newspaper, one of Granderson's special doughnuts that my mother-in-law was implicitly required to pick up on Fridays, and, even more exciting, Internet access.

I sat at their table, sampled an old-fashioned glazed doughnut, sipped on coffee, and perused the pitching matchups of my fantasy baseball team. I couldn't be better accommodated. I felt guilty, considering what was going on with Kiersten down the hallway, but who was I to complain if they wanted to take care of me?

And then things, as they always seemed to do, got terribly uncomfortable.

"Michael Charles!" my mother-in-law exclaimed as I was discovered in the break room. "Did Kiersten tell you what I got for you?"

Her joy disconcerted me. She was one for mischief. "Why…no… what did you get for me?"

"Oh, well, I just can't show you right now!" she said.

I could sense she was waiting for me to be playfully intrigued.

"Well, when can I expect to find out?"

"As soon as Kiersty-pie is done with Granderson and Ken," she said, whimsically clapping her hands in the air and kicking one leg awkwardly out to the side in celebration.

"I look forward to it…" I said.

Lord only knows what she has in store.

Ken greeted us in the break room, pulling his scrubs cap off his head. "Sixteen!" he said.

"Sixteen eggs?" I asked.

"Yep—they all look great," he said.

"Wow, that's outstanding."

"You can go see Kiersten if you'd like," he said.

Kiersten was still pretty groggy from the anesthesia, but she was surprisingly lucid in comparison to previous rounds.

"How did it go?" she asked.

"Sixteen, I hear."

"Wow."

"Yeah, nice work," I said. "You okay?

"A little out of it. Can you hand me that cup?"

I passed her a plastic cup with a splash of orange juice inside, designed to give her a few calories to bring her back into the world of the living. I couldn't help but wonder where she'd been for the last half hour. Anesthesia isn't a pain killer, it just sends you to another orbit while trained professionals do ungodly things to your body. Creepy.

"Now it's your turn, Michael, just grab the bag on the way in…" said Ken.

How do I always forget that I have to do this?

"Oh, Michael Charles!" exclaimed my mother-in-law. "Did Kiersten tell you about the present I have for you yet?"

I looked at Kiersten , who lightly shrugged her shoulders and rolled her eyes halfway into her lids. Or, at least, she moved in a subtle way that a person previously anesthetized would use to indicate they weren't going to tell you what you wanted to know. Kind of a post-coma don't-bother-me gesture.

"Why no, I don't think she did," I said.

"Well, I know how you've been displeased with our…um…selection," she said.

Oh boy…

"So I went into the 'Adult Shop' on the way to work today…"

Oh boy…

"…and I marched right in there and I told the woman at the front desk that I needed some dirty magazines for my son-in-law!"

"Oh my God, you didn't," I said.

"Oh, I DID!" she proclaimed excitedly. "They thought I was the greatest mother-in-law ever!"

"That you might be," I said.

She then delivered the goods. Six new dirty magazines for my collection-room pleasure. Not one, but *six*! This was a committed woman—or the suggestive selling at the Adult Shop was top-shelf.

"They said that you'd like this one." She gestured at a magazine with a bevy of scantily clad young ladies on the cover. "And then I told them that I needed a few more like this one, and they gave me the rest."

If you can possibly imagine how uncomfortable it is to have your mother-in-law purchasing pornography for you, you might be able to recreate the face I was making. I imagine it's similar to one you might make if your attractive cousin came on to you. Flattered, but…um… *"icky."*

On the one hand, I appreciated the gesture. Indeed, the 'inspirational' rags they had in the collection room were in desperate need of some upgrades, but why did it need to take place when I had to go in there—and why, *why* for the love of God did my mother-in-law have to be the one shopping for the goods?

She handed me a stack of magazines. "You just take these in there and do your business!" she said with a devilish grin.

She was taking sick pleasure in this.

258   MICHAEL C. BARR

I took the magazines and the bag including instructions and cup, and fled into the collection room, once again securing the door multiple times.

In my arms lay enough visual and journalistic depravity to land me in the slammer in Salt Lake City, no doubt. There were magazines featuring the young, the large, the "busty," the "uber-busty," the, ahem, "mature," and, yes, celebrities caught at inopportune moments. I'm not sure if Geena was in there, I didn't look at the whole thing. What was left was pretty much German and French girls — and I'm sure there was some kind of theme to these magazines, but I really couldn't figure it out beyond a general "yicky" principal. Whoever recommended these rags to my mother-in-law must have been one twisted individual. Or perhaps she described me as a sexually repressed person who was in dire need of images of hairy French women having an encounter with an inordinate number of buzzing accessories.

In sum, this was the most bizarre collection of magazines I'd ever seen in my adult life. But strangely, I appreciated the gesture so much that I felt an obligation to stay in the room long enough to sample the questionable content found therein. Or at the very least, to maintain the illusion that I was, indeed, using each and every sickening rag to satisfy myself. And so I disappeared behind the collection room door with my new half-dozen icky adult rags. Despite the fact that my true task was finished in no time (hey, they make us abstain for four days before a retrieval!), I spent enough time back there in order to say I'd seen at least one perverted photo from each of the magazines my mother-in-law had lovingly purchased for

me. I could only imagine how confused those who followed me in here would be when they found these x-
rated gems mixed in with Reagan-era soft porn. Maybe
there was a future for me in pornography-speculating for
infertility clinics across the globe. After all, I was going to
need to explore every last option to make a dime after
this business was done.

Having children is like having
a bowling alley installed in your brain.

– Martin Mull

I Would Not Like Them Here or There

The days following a retrieval were always fragile. This was when you learned the outcome of the eggs, which ones were usable, how many fertilized, and what the plans were for those that did. It was a strange thing to root for your body parts as they were being introduced to each other in an overheated lab, but that's exactly what you did.

In our case, our sixteen eggs quickly turned to eleven "injectable" eggs. As described by Ken, some of the eggs were too "hard," though I still have no damned idea how he could know that. Some time later, we discovered that Ken had actually tried to allow some sperm to fertilize a couple of eggs on their own, based on his notion that my sperm was now super-smoking-Courvoisier-drinking-ladies'-man-stud sperm. Turned out one of the eggs actually did fertilize "naturally" — without the ICSI process — but it let in two sperm, so it wasn't usable.

We referred to that one as "the slutty egg."

Ultimately, eleven eggs fertilized. Ken thought they all looked great, but he pulled out the four that looked best and decided to freeze the other seven. It was strange to know that those seven weren't likely to be thawed for a half-dozen years, if at all; if this round were to fail, it was adoption full steam ahead. We both figured we would go back to the frozen fertilized embryos at some point, but it certainly didn't seem to be our most fruitful path to parenthood. Ethical questions aside, it still posed very strange dilemmas—questions that FNBs never had to contemplate.

So the wait was officially on to see how those four chosen ones would proceed. Like last time, this was a "blastocyst" process, where the fertilized embryos were grown for five to six days and only the highest quality ones (assuming several of them actually progressed well enough) were transferred. We would know more in a couple of days, then hope to have at least two that "blasted."

In the meantime, it was my job to pursue the adoption process with full energy, stopping only to fill my wife's midsection with expensive prescription drugs each evening. Recognizing that the meeting with our social worker was near, I started to polish off my treatise of a personal questionnaire. I also broke down and made the appointment with my doctor for the mandated physical checkup, which I so loathed, and coordinated a notary to meet me there. This notary came recommended, so hopefully she would appear to have an IQ higher than my vacuum cleaner. I wondered if she would have to watch the doctor check my prostate. *"Could you notarize my ass while you're here?"*

Ken called on day three, post-transfer. The embryos "couldn't look better," he reported. He thought they would all go to blast on the fifth day, and encouraged us to clear our calendars for the transfer (they don't look at "blast" embryos on day four, since they apparently all look just terrible right before they mature). I realized I'd made my adoption doctor's appointment for day five, but I'd made it for the late afternoon since most transfers take place in the morning, so I decided I'd wait for the fifth day assessment before I rescheduled.

This round continued to feel so much more positive than the others. It seemed as if everything was going exactly according to plan. Despite our well-honed ability to be guarded and cautious throughout the trials of the last year, we both felt surprisingly optimistic. If I were a betting man, I'd definitely put my money on a positive result. Wait, I *was* putting money on this. But you get my point.

But then day five came.

Ken called with bad news. None of the embryos looked like they were ready to go to blast. One looked as if it wasn't going to survive much longer. He thought two others probably weren't going to make it, but he'd "keep watching them." The last one had a shot to go to blast, but it was maybe 50-50. Knowing Ken's assessments by now, I realized that he was typically a glass-half-full kind of guy, so this was particularly damning news. So maybe we'd do a transfer on day six.

Suddenly our fourth-round miracle turned into a fourth-round dud. However, Kiersten wasn't concerned — she was feeling the same way we had when we started this last round: whatever happens, happens. She had zero expectations for this round and was simply enduring the daily hormone injections to arrive at some degree of resolution — would it be biological first or adopted first?

But I was quite irritated. How could four top-shelf embryos look so great on day three and so shitty on day five? Did they need to improve the conditions back there? Was it too hot in Ken's House of Embryos? Was Ken drunk? (Okay, I knew Ken wasn't drunk…it was just fun to imagine.) But seriously, why was it that *our* embryos, which started out as top-shelf, high-quality fertilized eggs, turned out to be such underachievers?

"It's not going to work, is it?" Kiersten asked. "This is it."

"I don't know… it doesn't sound good," I said.

"Well, I don't want to transfer just one of those things tomorrow, so hopefully they all just putter out or a couple of them look great," she said.

Somehow, I knew it was going to be a fiasco either way, but I prayed that we got some kind of definitive resolution with this round, regardless. We'd know more in a day.

DAY FIVE

Since Ken had called so early on day five, I decided to go ahead and go into work. I also marked myself out on my calendar for the 4:00 o'clock appointment that I was *so looking forward to* with the doctor and notary, neither of whom I'd met before.

I arrived at the doctor's office at a quarter to four and scanned the waiting room. Nobody appeared to be a notary. I wasn't sure what I was looking for, but it typically involved repeated rocking back and forth and excessive drooling. Nobody fit that description.

I was anxious as I waited for the notary to arrive. Kiersten had borne the brunt of the adoption responsibilities and this was one of the main things over which I'd had total control. I was terrified I was going to screw it up. If I couldn't even handle this, how was I going to pass inspection by the social worker?

The nurse emerged from the saloon-style swinging doors and called my name. I asked her if she could wait a moment and asked the front desk person if she could give me the name of the woman the office had recommended as a notary when I made the original appointment. She gave me the 'are you a wacko?' look, so I explained my adoption situation. She then looked up my record and found the name of the notary to whom they had referred me. She gave me her number and I quickly dialed her up on my cell phone.

"Hello?" said the unassuming voice.

"Hi, uh…this is Michael Barr—I thought you might be meeting me at my doctor's appointment today to notarize my adoption paperwork?"

"Oh, um…no, I don't think so" she said. "Let me just check my sched… oh, dear. Yes… um…yes. Here it is. Oh, my gosh, I'm so sorry— I totally spaced the appointment. I'll be there in ten minutes."

Bring a rag for the drool.

"Okay, I'll probably be back with the doc. Just announce yourself at the front desk when you get here," I said.

I asked the receptionist if they would allow her to come back and she graciously obliged. I could sense the remainder of the waiting room figures angrily staring at me as if my antics would extend their wait. I nervously smiled at a couple of them, but I didn't imagine telling them my sperm don't swim well was particularly appropriate at the moment, despite the fact that it might buy me some sympathy.

"What are you looking at, Mr. Perfect Motility!"

I was escorted back to the room where they took my blood pressure and pulse, asked me a few healthy-lifestyle questions and then told me the doctor would "be here in a moment." I knew "a moment" meant sometime between now and next Tuesday, so I was confident the notary would be here by the time the doc arrived.

I was reading a stunning article about the precise time I should be digging up my dahlias and the exact temperature to store their root balls in *Sunset Magazine* when the notary appeared. She was unlike any notary I had encountered thus far. First of all, she appeared to be from this solar system. When she spoke it seemed she was also intelligent. She apologized profusely for her negligence with regard to the appointment and assured me she would do this notarization for free (it was to be a minimum of $45 dollars otherwise—just another way adoptive parents are gouged). We then engaged in a moderately sophisticated conversation about adoption. She told me about her acquaintances who were adopting from China, and I talked about our trials and tribulations in getting the paperwork finished. On the whole, I was quite pleased with her despite her tardiness.

There was a rap at the door.

"Yeah!" I spouted, figuring it was the doctor, finally working his way through all the hypochondriacs and elderly.

But this was a nurse. She had a note.

"Are you Michael?"

Oh, shit…what did I do? Was I supposed to get my parking validated?

"Yeeesss…" I said cautiously. I just knew if I'd screwed something up, the notary would surely reinstate her $45 fee.

The nurse handed me a scribbled note that read, "Your mother-in-law needs to speak with you—it's an emergency."

Oh, for crying out loud—what the hell now?

"Is there a problem?" asked the notary.

"Uh, no problem... I just need to step out for a minute," I said. "If the doc gets here, let him know I'll be just a minute." I walked down the hallway and called my mother-in-law.

"Hello?"

"Hey, it's Michael, what's up?"

"Michael Charles!" Karen said, panicked. "We've been trying to get a hold of Kiersten, but she isn't answering her phone!"

Figuring there was some kind of 'white sale' at Macy's that she didn't want Kiersten to miss, I responded with a degree of irritation. "Well, I'm here trying to get my doc's appointment notarized for the adoption, can't this wait?"

"But Michael Charles, you have embryos that need to be transferred right away!" she exclaimed.

"We do?!" I responded in total disbelief. "Whose are they?"

"This is no time for jokes, we need to get you here right away—Ken says they need to be transferred right now!" she said.

*   *   *

This is probably a good opportunity to tell you the background involved with this revelation regarding our embryos. This gets a little nutty, so bear with me...

After Ken called us the morning of day five, he apparently decided to check on the little budding monsters before the end of the day to see which ones were still kicking and which ones could be discarded. Upon scanning our four, he discovered an unexpected change. Three were at the brink of blast and the fourth was looking surprisingly good. They were too mature to wait till the sixth day—they needed to be transferred in the next couple of hours.

Ken hustled to the lobby to tell Karen that we needed to come in immediately for the transfer. So she called Kiersten but came up empty. Turns out, Kiersten didn't have her phone and we didn't have a "land line," just cell phones. So Karen called my work, where she left three increasingly panicked messages. Next was my cell, which I had turned off—since I was in an appointment with a physician.

Ken re-emerged. "Did you get in touch with them? We need them in here ASAP!"

"No! I'm trying!" Karen said.

"And where's Granderson?" Ken asked.

"Oh, no—he went golfing this afternoon when his calendar cleared!" she said.

Thinking quickly, Karen called my office back.

"I need to talk to Jeanne Ryan," she said.

Jeanne was one of our closest friends and happened to work with me. Unfortunately, her name wasn't Jeanne Ryan, it was Jeanne Gaffney. But her husband was named Ryan—so it was just the confluence of circumstances and a little bit of lunacy that caused Karen to ask for Jeanne Ryan instead.

"There's nobody that works here by that name," our dutiful front-desk person responded.

"I *know* you have a Jeanne Ryan that works there! She's tall and blonde…"

"May I ask who is calling?" our front desk person appropriately asked.

"I'm the mother-in-law of Michael Barr and it's very important that I talk with Jeanne Ryan right away!"

"Well… we have a Jeanne *Gaffney* who works here, is that who you were thinking of?"

"Oh, YES! JEANNE GAFFNEY! Please put me through!"

Happy to unload another mildly insane caller, the receptionist transferred my mother-in-law back to Jeanne.

Now, Jeanne was one of the few who knew about our procreation high-jinks, so it didn't take Karen long to explain why it was important that she find one of us very soon. Ever resourceful, Jeanne checked my calendar, where she discovered my doctor's appointment with Dr. Adrian. All that was left was for Karen to look up a Dr. Adrian and try to convince the staff to ignore every privacy regulation in the world and relay an urgent message to me.

Unfortunately, when I made the appointment, it was with a doctor I'd never seen before. When they told me his name, I just guessed at the spelling and put that on my calendar. His name wasn't Adrian, it was Dr. Adrience. How was I supposed to know this would be a life-changing phonetic decision?

Needless to say, when Karen went to the phone book to look him up, there was no Dr. Adrian.

She tried Kiersten's cell phone again and got her all-too-familiar peppy voice-message, *"Hi, you've ALMOST reached Kiersten—leave a message and I'll call you back!"*

Karen's message was practically unintelligible.

Her last resort was to consult the white pages. She ran through the phone book, looking for anyone that resembled a Dr. Adrian. Believe it or not, she found a doctor named Dr. Adrien.

She frantically dialed the number and started rehearsing what her rationale to the nurse was going to be.

Disconnected.

Beginning to reach, she started calling local health organizations at random, asking if they had a Dr. Adrian. One of the outfits said they knew a Dr. *Adrience*, who was a roving physician in the county—they thought he was working with Pacific Family Medicine this week.

Gold.

She looked them up and dialed as fast as her digits allowed.

"Pacific Family Medicine, how can I help you?"

"Hello, this is Karen calling from North Sound In-Vitro Fertilization, do you have a patient there with you today named Michael Barr?" she asked. She knew full well they couldn't reveal this information.

"I'm sorry, we can't disclose that information…"

"Yes, I know, but it's urgent that I get a message to him," she said.

I'll remind you that I was the very patient who had to ask the staff to look up my record to find the notary who stood me up, called her while I irritated nurses and patients alike, and then asked the staff to refer her back to my room when she arrived. Now my mother-in-law was calling, asking them to break basic privacy laws to communicate an urgent message to me. It was a miracle they didn't accidentally prescribe an impromptu colonoscopy for me that evening.

"Ma'am, you know I can't…"

"Yes, I know," Karen said. "But can you just give him a note, *if he happens to be there*, that asks him to call his mother-in-law? It is extremely urgent!"

Savvy thinking by the mom-in-law, really.

The receptionist stewed for a while. She put her on hold and consulted a nurse. "Okay, we'll deliver that message, *if he's here for an appointment*."

Gotta love the language of covering one's ass.

With that duck lined up, she needed to find Granderson on the links. Fortunately for them, he always played the same course, as he was a member at the local country club (I always say 'local country club' like Mr. Howell from *Gilligan's Island*, jaw protruding and arrogance thick).

Like all good docs, Granderson had his cell phone on, even at the course.

"Hello," he said, irritably.

"Dr. Granderson—Kiersten and Michael's embryos are blasting!" she said.

"But I'm one under after eight holes!" he groaned.

"GRANDERSON, YOU GET IN HERE RIGHT NOW, MY GRANDCHILDREN ARE WAITING!"

"Call me when they're on their way and I'll leave immediately," he said.

*   *   *

So that brings us to my current conversation.

"Okay, I'll figure out a way to get Kiersten there as soon as possible," I said to Karen. "We'll get there, don't worry."

I called Kiersten.

"Hi, you've ALMOST reached Kiersten…"

Oh, shut up. Where the hell are you?! I hit the "#" button, which sent me straight to voice mail.

"Hey lady, you better find your phone, we've apparently got some kids that want the chance to grow in your uterus—call me as soon as you get this."

I saw the doctor approach the room in which I'd just been waiting with my notary. He looked at me, curious who this idiot on the cell phone in the hallway was. I had to say something, didn't I?

"Hi, are you Doctor Adrian?"

"Adrience," he said with a tone so pensive, it could only be achieved by someone with a medical license.

"I'm Michael Barr, you're supposed to be seeing me in there, but it's just my notary in there right now."

He cocked his head to the right, like a chocolate lab might when asked if he wanted to go on a walk.

And then I delivered a most satisfying line. I held up my index finger and said, "I'll be with you in just a minute."

Clearly confused, he maintained eye contact with me as he slowly opened the door and backed into the examination room, clutching his clipboard. A part of me wanted to give them a half hour in there together as payback for all the countless hours I'd spent waiting for physicians.

I decided to call our neighbor.

"Steve, it's Michael."

"Hey, man—what's going on?" he said.

"Well, I have a favor to ask."

"Oh, yeah?"

Typically, a favor involved milling us something in his shop or helping me load something into the truck for a run to the dump. I'm not sure Steve was prepared for my request.

"I need to you grab the spare key to our house and get in there and find my wife," I said.

"Uhh…" he muttered.

"Yeah, I know this is weird, but I need you to find her and tell her to call her mother," I said. "I can't really explain why, but I think she's either taking a nap or is in the shower or something. I just need you to bust in there and find her. If you don't find her, please call me back."

"Uhh, okay…"

He was not at all comfortable with finding my naked or half-naked napping wife, but I didn't have time to explain the complicated situation we were facing just now. As always, though, Steve delivered.

I approached my examination room, and couldn't help but give the proverbial "knock knock" that the doc always gave before storming in. *I so want to ask a nurse for someone's chart. STAT!*

"Hi, sorry about that—I uh, well… I'm just having a very strange day."

"Do you have the adoption paperwork that I'm supposed to cover?" my new doc asked abruptly as he stared into his laptop computer. He was clearly irritated.

"Yeah, of course." I handed him the information that he needed to fill out.

"Okay, we've got your blood pressure and your height and weight here already…I need to ask you some general health questions…" he said.

"Fire away."

He started asking me about exercise, family health history, how much I drank (how proud was I to say "one per day" for the first time in my adult life?), whether or not I took any illicit drugs, among many other assorted inquiries.

"Okay, I just have a couple more … "

"Oh, Doctor," the notary interrupted.

"Yes?" he said, with a 'what the *hell* do you want' look on his face.

"Technically, I should have sworn you in before you asked all of those questions," she said.

Silence ensued. I thought the doc was about to get up and leave, while I was just shocked that I'd witnessed a notary use a four-syllable word.

"But considering the circumstances here, I can just do it now," she said.

"Okay. Fine," he said, steam starting to trickle out of his ears.

"Raise your right hand and repeat after me," she said.

Oh, man, I think he's going to punch her.

He raised his hand in a bit of a mocking flap upward and rather sarcastically repeated her words.

My eyes widened and shifted back and forth between the two, wagering in my head who might crack first.

Two to one that the doc gets up and leaves.

Four to one that the doc swears out loud that this is the most absurd thing he's ever been a part of.

Eight to one that we see punches.

Ten to one that the notary wets herself. Any takers?

Fortunately for all parties, we survived the doctor's appointment, I had my paperwork notarized and I didn't even have to pay a dime.

I turned on my phone as soon as I handed over my co-pay. Four messages.

Skipping over the first three that started out, "MICHAEL CHARLES!", I got to the fourth, which was Kiersten letting me know that her mother was coming to pick her up and she'd meet me at the clinic.

*   *   *

"So, Michael Charles," Granderson said. "I was even par after ten holes when Karen pulled me off the course."

"Wow, that's impressive," I said. "Did you know that we're zero for three for in-vitro?"

"Point taken," he said. "We're going to fix that today."

Kiersten walked through the door with her mother. She was greeted by me, Granderson, Ken, and Linda. The entire office was standing in the lobby, waiting for their single patient for the day. Talk about customer service.

Ken was clearly relieved to see his patient at long last. "Okay, let's get those embryos transferred finally!" he said.

We all walked together back to the chili-dog room without delay. The panel came off, Ken's House of Embryos was revealed, and the transfer was on in no time.

The last round of in-vitro, underway.

And finally, I exhaled.

When I consider how little of a rarity children are—that every street and blind alley swarms with them—that the poorest people commonly have them in most abundance—that there are few marriages that are not blest with at least one of these bargains—how often they turn out ill, and defeat the fond hopes of their parents, taking to vicious courses, which end in poverty, disgrace, the gallows, etc. —I cannot for my life tell what cause for pride there can possibly be in having them.

– Charles Lamb (1775-1834)

No Fooling

I was sitting next to Kiersten in the chili-dog room as we waited out the customary hour before she was allowed to get up and move around. We needed to give our little babies an opportunity to get in there and take hold.

"Well, they're all in there, so you guys just rest up for a while and I'll come check on you in a bit," said Linda. She dimmed the lights and closed the door behind her. A peaceful quiet settled into the room. The hum of the barely-lit florescent lights above was soothing. I was exhausted from the events of this insane day. I contemplated putting my head down on Kiersten's stomach to nap for the hour.

I leaned my face toward her belly. "Hello in there," I said softly. "It would be great if one of you could stick around this time. You kids can rock-paper-scissors for who gets to implant, okay?"

I got a little chuckle from Kiersten, which was okay with me—we didn't need any belly laughs after the transfer.

We were both silent and calm for what felt like a half hour. The heat from Ken's House of Embryos behind that chili-dog window must have been seeping in, because it was about 75 degrees. I was fading in and out of consciousness.

"I wonder how many they wound up transferring?" Kiersten said.

"What do you mean?" I asked.

"Well, Linda said 'they're all in there.' We never really had a discussion about how many they were putting in."

I was awake now.

"I think you're probably reading too much into what she said," I said. "Didn't we transfer two last time?"

"Yeah, but I wanted them to transfer three," she said. "And remember they said they would *never* transfer three during a 'blast' round because of the risk of triplets."

"Oh yeah—so I'm sure they transferred two this time."

"Yeah, probably two," she concurred.

We fell silent again, but this stillness didn't feel peaceful. I was fairly sure Kiersten was freaking out just as much as I was, not knowing what they had just inserted into her uterus. We trusted the staff so much at this point, they could have put a bucket of fried chicken up there and we wouldn't have noticed.

Linda knocked on the door and poked her head in. "Everything okay in here? Can I get you anything?"

"I'm okay," Kiersten said. "But I have an embarrassing question to ask you."

"What's that?" asked Linda.

"How many did they transfer?"

"You don't know?"

"No, they didn't really discuss it with us."

"I'll ask Ken," she said, slowly closing the door and making a face that suggested we were already bad parents.

"I'm sure it's two, babe," I said. "They would have told us if they did more, right? Hell, it's probably more likely they did one than *three*."

"You're probably right," she said.

We sat and stewed while Linda investigated, quietly consumed by this ridiculous mystery of how many five-day fertilized embryos were inside Kiersten. I wasn't sure this day could get any more bizarre.

Linda knocked.

"Yes?" said Kiersten.

Linda poked her head in. Following her head was her hand. On her hand were three extended fingers. "*Three*," she mouthed, looking a little surprised herself.

"Thanks, Linda," Kiersten said graciously.

The door closed. Kiersten and I both extended eyes-bulged stares at each other.

Three? Seriously…THREE?

"I'm going to go talk to Ken," I said. "You and the triplets hang tight."

"Very funny."

I headed down the hallway and made a familiar turn past the collection room, where the door was wide open. I sympathetically looked at the couch. I momentarily considered donating it to Goodwill so it could finish its life with a nice family, or at the very least to some college kids, where it would get doused with beer and be crashed upon by strangers.

"Ken!"

"Yeah, everything okay?" he asked.

"Uh—so you guys decided to transfer three, huh?"

"You didn't know that?"

"No."

"Yeah, we transferred three."

"No fooling," I said.

"No fooling," he said.

I nervously nodded my head repeatedly and stared at him, like a stunned bobble-head doll on a dashboard. My look said, "*So, Ken, I should come to you for a loan when my wife births triplets?*"

"So I assume a couple were of decent quality and the third was just kind of a toss-in?" I asked.

"No, they all looked fantastic," he said. "Granderson felt comfortable with three based on your history."

"But you once told us that you would *never* transfer three during a 'blast' round."

"Well, we do now."

"I guess you do."

I smiled uncomfortably. It could have easily been construed as a grimace. It was the same look I used to give people when they approached the counter to purchase an O-Town CD back when I worked at a music store. *You sure you want to do that?*

I guess this wasn't O-Town, though. This was my life. Those were my children. But mark my words, if three of those kids popped out and formed a boy band, I was going to be really freaking pissed.

Seeing my cranks turning, Ken told me everything was going to work out great. That there was a really small chance of triplets. He added, "Of course, one of the embryos could always split, so I guess I should tell you there's an even smaller chance of getting quads, huh?"

Ken laughed, amused at his own syllogism.

I almost threw up.

I returned to the chili-dog room before Ken could get to the odds of five or six.

"Well?" said Kiersten.

Find your center… find your center… deep breath…

"Ken says everything will be fine," I said. "The hour is up, you want to go home?"

"Yeah—I'm ready," she said. "I'm so glad I'll never have to do this again."

"I don't blame you," I said. "I'm glad your mother will never buy me porn again."

We slowly meandered through the office and exited the building. Kiersten, me, and the triplets.

*   *   *

The day after the transfer, we were both resting comfortably per the doc's instructions. Well, Kiersten was resting and I was pretty much waiting on her, but that's okay—I wasn't the one sitting there waiting for an embryo to implant in my womb. I was just about to fetch some New Peking takeout when Ken called.

"Your fourth blasted," he said.

As this was not the typical salutation, I didn't immediately understand what he was saying. "Huh?" I intelligently replied.

"Your fourth embryo—the one that we didn't think would survive. It went to blast today."

"Oh! Is that good?" I asked for probably the four hundredth time during this preposterous procreation pursuit.

"Yeah, of course it's good," Ken said. "If this was the one that looked the worst, then the others should have a very good chance."

I glanced at Kiersten's stomach to see if she was already looking pregnant.

"Who was that?" she asked.

"Ken."

"What's up?"

"Well, apparently the fourth one went to blast."

"You're kidding me."

"Nope."

"So the three inside me have a really good chance of continuing, don't they?" she said, borderline rhetorically.

"Apparently," I said.

"Perfect," she said.

There we were, thigh-deep in the adoption process, already having fallen in love with some little girl who was a six-pack of Tsingtao away from conception, and now we had three ringers growing in Kiersten's tummy. *Of course* we were going to get a positive now. *Of course* we were going to get multiples now. *Of course* it was going to complicate the path that we'd invested in now.

"Not to add injury to the insult…" I said, "but it's time for your shot."

"I hate these fucking shots," she said.

Now that's the kind of spunk I like to hear.

REAL BABY

"HI MIKE, HI KURSTEN!!!" Jessica greeted us as we entered New Peking. My mouth had started watering in the parking lot, where you could smell the cholesterol-spiking dishes before you got out of your car.

"Hi, Jessica," I said.

"YOU SIT ANYWHERE YOU LIKE."

"We're just here for take out," I said.

"OH, I GET SAM FOR YOU."

I wasn't sure if they had a bed installed behind the register—sort of like how George Costanza had a napping nook engineered under his desk at Yankee Stadium— but once again, from beneath the counter emerged little Breanna.

"Five!" she said, her hand outstretched with all fingers extended.

"You're five?" asked Kiersten.

Breanna nodded.

"When is your birthday?" I asked.

She started bouncing up and down, hopping around like a bunny, then paused and scrunched her nose up as if she was smelling something bad, and laughed. It would have been cute, but she was laughing and pointing at me.

"Did I say something funny?" I asked Kiersten.

Now Kiersten was laughing at me.

I don't think I'm going to understand fatherhood very much.

Sam emerged from the depths of Mongolian Beef-dom. He saw Breanna laughing and pointing at me, Kiersten laughing at me (*with me*, she would later argue) and me scratching my head. He interpreted this as me playing with Breanna, apparently.

"Time for you!" he said, gesturing to Breanna. "Time for you! Time to have baby! Time running out!"

Sam apparently didn't realize Tony Randall fathered a baby at 77. I think I've got time.

"Actually," Kiersten interjected, "we have some news for you, Sam."

Sam's eyes got big.

"We're adopting from China."

"What?" he asked.

"We're adopting a baby—from China!" she said.

"Baby from China! Oh this is good! This is good, good!" he said.

"We're pretty excited," said Kiersten.

"First you adopt, then you have REAL BABY!" said Sam, gesturing with his hand over his stomach, in the international sign of being pregnant.

I lost it. My laughter bellowed uncontrollably. Laughing *with her*, I'd later argue.

Kiersten came to the rescue of our adopted kid. "So an adopted baby from China isn't a real baby, Sam?" she asked.

"Oh, you know—real baby!" he said as he re-enacted the big prego belly.

"I think you mean a biological baby, right?" said Kiersten

"Yes, yes! Bi-oh-logical!" said Sam.

What a spectacle we must have been—Sam continuing to do the international pregnant motion with his arms, his daughter Breanna hopping around the entry, holding her nose and pointing at me, my wife trying to bridge the language gap with Sam, while I couldn't stop laughing.

"I'm FIVE," yelled Breanna—it seemed the focus wasn't on her quite enough and this was the surest thing she could holler to get my attention.

"Yep, you're five. And apparently I stink."

JUST ONE

This fourth round had been a real mind job.

First, this round practically ended our marriage, then it gave us hope. Then everything looked great with the embryos, then they looked horrible, then fantastic. And then the clinic decided to cast aside their typical practice and transfer enough embryos to turn a traditional 4-6-3 double play.

And now I sat here at my desk—a panicked twitching idiot waiting for Kiersten to call. She was getting a blood test at this very moment.

I'd gnawed my fingernails down to nubs.

I'd picked at the dry skin around my thumbnails until one started to bleed (ick, I know).

I'd started to pull at my eyebrows and I was worried that I might have plucked one bald.

As I stared catatonically into my computer screen, an e-mail popped up, inviting me to a co-worker's baby shower. They needed someone to bring napkins and cheesecake.

Fucking perfect.

I considered attending in a T-shirt with a silk-screened middle finger and text reading, "I CAN'T MAKE BABIES."

The enormity of the present situation was consuming me. I couldn't help but become absorbed with our potential outcomes. No, I didn't really want three babies— but I'd take three over none. Frankly, I wasn't so sure we could even handle twins—but I'd be absolutely thrilled if there were two in there. Please God, don't even make me think about the possibility of four. Hmm … I just did it. Arrgh … I just did it again.

But really, what was wrong with one?

Just … one.

Four rounds of in-vitro fertilization, thousands of dollars, a year of our lives consumed with indescribable emotional duress. Was one too much to ask for?

I was trying to focus on my job, but this was a colossal distraction. I'd essentially come down with in-vitro-induced adult attention deficit disorder.

My phone rang.

Don't we deserve one? Just one?

But then what about adoption? Would we still go through with it right away, or would we wait? I really don't want to wait …

Second ring.

The reality of what this phone call meant struck me.

This call will tell me if I'll ever have a biological kid.

It had never really occurred to me like that. It wasn't that my whole identity relied on having a kid that looked like me, because I really didn't think I cared about that. But when something you'd taken as such a given, that *someday* I would produce a child, when that was hanging in the balance, it was an extremely odd realization.

The phone rang again. I had one more ring before it went to voice mail.

I might never produce a biological child.

But I know I will be a good father.

And I know I will love my kids with everything I have in my heart and mind, regardless of how they got here.

I grabbed the receiver, pulled it up, and took a full, pronounced breath.

"Hello?"

"Looks like we're going to China," Kiersten said.

"So... nothing?" I said

"Nope."

"God. How can that... it's so... it's just..." I stuttered.

"It just wasn't meant to be," she said, emotionless and faint.

We both paused. My head fell in my hand. I uttered the only thing I could think to say.

"You okay?"

"Yeah, I'm fine," she said. "I'm already looking forward to the adoption. Are you okay?"

"Yeah. Fine."

Truth was, I was hurt. I was confused. But I wasn't devastated.

I was more amazed that despite each enormous letdown, I'd allowed myself to think we'd be successful every time thereafter. Four times now. I started to wonder if there was an island in the Pacific that a traveling salesman would soon pitch me.

Kurt Vonnegut once wrote that humor is a way of holding off how awful life can be in order to protect yourself, and that ultimately you may just get too tired, and the news is too awful, and humor doesn't work anymore. I could finally relate to that. I couldn't think of anything funny to rationalize this, to give it perspective. I was without words; a numbness of wit enveloped me. I was emotionally immobile.

I felt gullible.

I hadn't learned anything from the previous hurt.

I hadn't protected myself.

And yet, I felt a sense of relief just to know what my future held. The uncertainty was completely gone—our path couldn't have been more obvious. And it was east. Very east.

"Well, I guess we can finally schedule the meetings with the social worker, huh?" I said.

"I'm calling as soon as I get home," Kiersten said.

Back when we first started talking about adoption, I had started looking over Chinese culture-related literature. I was reminded of a traditional Chinese proverb I'd found:

Man's schemes are inferior to those made by heaven.

I'd always tried to ignore it until now. We were clearly not designed for baby making and were compelled to adopt internationally—we'd meddled enough with manipulating our natural biology and it was unmistakably time to take what the Big Guy was driving us towards.

But then again, I also saw this one:

Your neighbor's wife looks prettier than your own.

I'm not sure what kind of lesson that one was trying to convey—maybe it was just the title of some kind of Qing Dynasty Jerry Springer show where a sword fight ensued.

But the point was, we had seen the process through as far as we could—or at least as far as our emotions and bank account could handle. Turning the page was both painful and cathartic.

China, here come the Barrs.

Please stock up on Mongolian Beef. And try to forget that some people no like baby.

Having children makes you no more a parent
than having a piano makes you a pianist.

– Michael Levine

THE GATEKEEPER

There would be five initial meetings with our social worker—two with the both of us, one with Kiersten, one with me, and then a home visit. If things worked out, she'd come back after we adopted and do a final assessment—just to make sure she wasn't duped, apparently.

I was nervous about the whole social worker thing. I envisioned meeting with a woman who resembled Tammy Faye Bakker or Sally Struthers, with massive hair-sprayed motionless blonde hair, copious makeup, and a permanent smile gracing her well-glossed lips. Her office would smell like a combination of cheap perfume and Sanka. The office building would feel like a legal firm with lots of well dressed people scuttling about with papers in their hands and serious faces. The social worker would have a corner office with plenty of light and her furniture would be oversized brown leather in which guests would attempt to relax and respond to her questions about why they were good candidates and how they planned to care for an adopted child. The interviews would be painful. She would interrogate us and attempt to peer into our souls, culling out dirty, dark secrets that would render us unfit to parent.

My expectations and overactive imagination were soon greeted by reality.

The office was in a downtown building in which neither of us had ever been— probably because there was no restaurant or bar inside. As we navigated up the uncommonly wide, steep stairs to the second floor, it was as if we were entering into a fog of stale cigarette smoke and mildew. This wasn't the odor of Sanka—definitely not perfume.

The hallways were unusually narrow. The carpet was stained with a variety of unknown liquids. We walked past a maze of nondescript windowless office doors. I discovered that in this bizarre, smelly, unsafe-seeming building, you could get legal advice, get your nails done, buy comic books, and plan an international vacation—and that was just one hallway of dozens. Our social worker's office was adjacent to the nail shop, which had an overpowering chemical odor of its own emanating from underneath the door.

We were greeted by Janet, our social worker. She stood about five feet high and resembled a prototypical elementary school librarian. Her warmth was immediate as she welcomed us in with a wide, genuine smile beneath her oversized thick glasses. The room was roughly 12 by 8, its walls adorned by posters of countries we'd never see. There was a small play-station for toddlers, complete with picture books and blocks. The room was dimly lit and probably about 83 degrees, "the warmest office in the building," she would soon boast. Two couches were flanked by a cork board littered with pictures resembling a homicide detective's wall of suspects, except these photos featured diverse families and toothy grins.

On the whole, we lucked out with Janet. She was the mother of three adopted children, and she also knew the process in China well, so she could cater her home study report to anticipate their requirements. Our meetings with her were extremely comfortable as she asked general questions about our marriage and our anticipated parenting style, and re-hashed our monstrous autobiographies with us — which was fine until she asked for clarification to one of my responses. Apparently, one of my wisecracks had slipped through.

"Michael, I see you answered the question regarding how you found out about sex…"

Oh, shit.

"…by answering, 'trial and error'?" she asked inquisitively.

"I wrote that?"

"Yes, it's right here. I wonder if you can help me understand what you mean by that?" she asked.

Kiersten looked at me, smiling. It was the "you wrote it, jackass, now deal with the consequences" look.

"Well, I never really got 'the talk,'" I said. "So I had to kind of feel my way around."

Crap. Did I just say 'feel my way around' in reference to sex?

"…well, not really 'feel my way' you know…uh…but. I… I uh… you know— never really…" I started nervously tapping the tips of my fingers together in my lap and squinting, as if preparing to be hit by an oncoming dodge ball.

"I think I understand," she said.

"Oh, THANK GOD—thank you!" I exhaled, exasperated.

Lesson learned—no sarcasm with Janet.

"Now, there's just one more thing you'll need to do for the home study, Michael," she said.

Please tell me you want me to fix your radiator—I'm burning up in here.

"You'll need to write a letter to address your little run-in with the law."

I had disclosed on the questionnaire that I once received a "Minor in Possession of Alcohol" citation when I was 18.

"But the questionnaire asked if I've ever been arrested, and I haven't," I said defensively. "That was just a citation, like a parking ticket, and it was lifted from my record when I turned 21 because I never got in trouble again." I didn't mention that I had simply learned to establish an early exit strategy at each and every college party I went to until I was 21, but I wasn't sure Janet, let alone China, needed to know that.

"Everything in your background will turn up at Immigration Services, and if you don't disclose something like this, it could disqualify you completely," she said.

"Wonderful," I muttered. "So what's this letter supposed to say?"

"Just provide some background and say that you're sorry and you learned your lesson," she said. "That's all they'll be looking for—but you need to address it."

"They want to know that I learned from getting busted drinking beer 15 years ago?" I asked. "Don't you think the lessons gleaned from that have long been spent?"

My hand suddenly felt great pressure. Kiersten was sending me an undisputable nonverbal message: *"SHUT UP."*

"I'll e-mail you the letter tomorrow."

*   *   *

I sat down as soon as we got home to hammer out this ridiculous explanation letter.

> *To Whom It May Concern:*
> *Fifteen years ago, I was cited for drinking Miller Genuine Draft with a bunch of my underage buddies. Today, I regret that decision.*
> *I should have chosen Bridgeport Brewery instead.*

That was clearly not going to work.

> *To Whom It May Concern:*
> *Fifteen years ago, I was cited for drinking beer in a large and unruly college party. There were drinking games going on, loud music, and attractive college-aged girls dancing and flirting with me.*
> *I learned from this experience. I never missed another party.*

"Man, college was fun," I sighed.

After a couple more of these ridiculous efforts, I finally got serious and cranked out a page-long letter about the context of the infraction, how it was an immature decision, and that I learned from it and have avoided trouble ever since.

It was the most accurate of the bunch, but not nearly as much fun to write.

I went to the kitchen and opened a beer before sending the letter off to Janet. All this taking responsibility made me thirsty.

PAGING CHAIRMAN MAO

One of the great joys in my life became telling someone that I was adopting a baby from China. The reaction you got from people was unequivocal enthusiasm. I'd never seen anything else quite like it. I was consistently surprised by the magnanimity and overall interest people displayed when we made our plans public to friends and acquaintances (and if you were Kiersten, sometimes to complete strangers). Each and every person we told reacted as if it was the best news they'd heard all year. Some people were even brought to tears.

What a strange thing, really. Were people just that empathetic to the plight of orphaned girls in China? Did they know about our struggles with infertility? Were they collectively feigning interest?

But it was great to celebrate the fact that our baby was on her way and our friends were excited right along with us.

Of course, there were a couple of people who had the balls to ask if we couldn't "have one of our own," but we got pretty good at responding, "Well, she will be our own, won't she?" That shut people up pretty fast. Or, since I was back on the sauce, after a couple of Imperial IPAs I was known to tell people to stick something large and uncomfortable up their rectum—which had the same kind of effect, but I guess it wasn't nearly as gentlemanly.

But now that we had our parenthood marching orders, the challenge was to navigate our way through the expanse of paperwork required to adopt.

Several things were being demonstrated with this paperwork. First, we were being evaluated as individuals on a "fit to be a parent" kind of scale. Next, we needed to prove we were healthy enough and that we had the means to provide for the kid. Lastly, we needed to file proper paperwork to bring an orphan here. Fair enough. The effort to satisfy all of these examinations would be reflected in our adoption dossier—the massive package of materials that we would send to our adoption agency, which would be translated, and sent across the Pacific to The People's Republic of China.

The dossier needed to include the following: an adoption petition, both of our birth certificates, marriage certificate, employment verification, financial statement, physical exams and blood work, police report and background checks, an approved United States Center for Immigration Services form I-171 (petition to bring an orphan to the United States), three "couple photos" (shots of us), eight "family life" photos (pictures of us with friends, out doing things we enjoy, etc.; we probably should have been honest and just sent pictures of Kiersten eating and me drinking beer), three passport photos, and of course, a completed, and ostensibly favorable, home study report.

That list might sound a little daunting, but it actually got worse. Each piece of paper needed to be notarized. I've already covered my general feelings about notaries and the notarization process. But the notarization wasn't enough—the notary then needed to be certified by the corresponding Secretary of State where the notarization took place (which could be challenging if you were, say, born in Massachusetts or Oregon, like my wife and I. So the notarization of our birth certificates needed to be FedExed with paid return FedEx envelopes to the corresponding states—which cost $30 per mailing, no less).

But wait, there's more.

After certification, the corresponding regional Chinese embassy needed to authenticate that the Secretary of State's name on the documents was, indeed, correct, which would make their certification of the notarization legitimate. To recap in idiot-speak: they check the checker who checked the notary, who checked your documents. A quadruple guarantee.

Who the heck was going to have final say that this stuff wasn't phony? I kept waiting for the need to ask God Himself to give approval to the embassy that endorsed the Secretary of State who authenticated the notarization, which made our paperwork official.

And as if this process wasn't ridiculous enough, we were also nickel-and-dimed to death along the way. The notarizations had a fee. The certifications had a fee, plus overnight mail expenses. The authentications were on a "fee-by-seal" basis, with most seals running $20 each, and many seals required a "handling fee" which varied in price, but none of them were cheap. We had 13 seals in all.

Hear that sucking sound? That's my bank account. But at least when the seals came back from the embassy, they looked cool—rice paper with some unintelligible red waxy stamp (intelligible if you spoke Mandarin, I suppose). Cool enough that it felt like you were getting something for the money.

We knew about the big-ticket expenses of adoption, but damn if the little ones didn't add up. But I guess that would imply that we planned for any of the expenses, which would be a complete lie.

The great China chase, however, was officially on. Based on our agency estimates, they were currently matching couples with babies after eight to ten months (that's *after* the dossier was received by the Chinese). Kiersten feverishly completed forms, scheduled appointments, and mailed papers to their appropriate locations. She made checklists, gave me assignments, dutifully assembled necessary documents, and set goals for when each step of the process should be completed.

"Janet said this might take four months, but I think we can get everything done in three," she said.

I wasn't going to argue with a tidal wave.

"Yeah, she's never seen the likes of you."

"I bet she hasn't!"

It wasn't really a compliment, but the obsessive-compulsive in Kiersten took it that way. And frankly, without her, this process would still be going on to this day. Alone, I'd have flown to China to get my baby by the time I qualified for Social Security. But my wife was built for gargantuan tasks requiring hyper-organization skills, especially when she wanted something.

We couldn't balance our checkbook to save our lives, but nothing would keep her from adopting a little girl from the other side of the planet.

FINGER POINTING

"You'll want to wear gloves with Vaseline inside," Janet said.

I stared at her, doing everything in my power to control the laughter boiling up inside me.

"Um, excuse me?" I said, a slight grin crossing my lips.

"Yeah, you know—you'll want to squeeze some petroleum jelly or Vaseline into latex gloves and wear them for about an hour a day the week before you get fingerprinted."

Kiersten and I nodded approvingly, both mortified. I was pretty sure Kiersten was quietly praying that I didn't ask something along the lines of, "What if I just used latex condoms on every finger in lieu of gloves, you know—since we really won't be needing all those rubbers we've got around the house?" (Incidentally, how thrilled was I that I'd never have to bother with a vasectomy!) But after the incident with the questionnaire, I was doing everything I could to control the sarcasm.

This was our last meeting with the social worker before she did the official "home visit." She was wrapping up our conversation by giving us tips for our trip to the Center for

Immigration Services, where we would need to apply for the I-171, the petition to bring an orphan into the United States. We would also need to get fingerprinted.

"You can't have any nicks or cuts on your fingers or else it will foul up the whole application process," she said. "The electronic fingerprinting machines are very fickle, so your fingerprints need to be in perfect shape— you can't have any blemishes on the pads of your fingers." Her slippery little solution to the fingerprinting hurdle was to sit around watching television with latex gloves filled with greasy personal lubricant.

And here I thought all the embarrassing shit was behind us.

"Well, help me understand what constitutes a 'bad' fingerprint," I requested.

"Anything that breaks the line of a fingerprint—so any nick, any scab, any tiny little cut on the pads of your fingers will mean that you'll have to be re-fingerprinted at a later date," she said. "And that will delay the paperwork."

This was not good news. I looked down at my fingers and counted four cuts and a variety of miscellaneous abrasions.

With all of the home projects and yard work that I had going on, my fingers were hammered. But regardless of the home-improvement mishaps, the truth was I was terribly accident prone, so it didn't take much for me to cut a finger. I could scarcely get dressed in the morning without banging my hand on something bad enough to draw blood. I was a lot like my Dad that way—he used to say that before he started a project, he'd just cut his finger and put a band-aid on it so that he wouldn't be interrupted by cutting it later.

I'd be damned if I'm going to sit around with latex gloves filled with Vaseline on, though. What if a drinking buddy showed up to discover that scene? First I stopped drinking with them, and now I was sitting there with KY-filled rubber gloves on? To further alienate myself from my friends, I might as well just tell them I was a vegan, I was joining the Jehovah's Witnesses, my new name was "Cosmo," and I only referred to myself in the third person.

"Cosmo needs to refill his Vaseline."

The only solution was to heal up the wounds I currently had and to be extra careful until we get to the Center for Immigration Services. We'd have grass that was four feet high, but my cuticles would be immaculate.

* * *

Weeks of filing adoption paperwork, having it notarized, certified, and authenticated bought my tender little fingers some time to recondition themselves. Janet had just finished the home study, which meant we were near the point of completing roughly three months of paper pushing. Assuming she was planning on giving us her okay, despite what had to be misgivings about my maturity level, we would have the final piece of paperwork necessary to file the I-171. So Kiersten and I both coordinated a day off work, during which we would drive roughly four hours to complete the process.

It took just a week for our home study to arrive in the mail. Janet had given us the official approval we needed. In her home study, she had described me as a "quiet, gentle, and thoughtful man," which I appreciated, since "terrified and sophomoric" was what I was expecting.

The home study was one of the last big items we'd needed for the dossier, and it completed what we would need to petition for the I-171. It felt like we had taken one giant step closer to concluding the adoption process. So we decided to celebrate.

Our friends Vince and Kara invited us over for dinner, and I decided to bring a couple of bottles of wine to mark the end of our paperwork process (okay, we still had a few steps, but who's counting). It was because of Vince and Kara that we were at all close to parenthood, as we were the godparents of their twins, Lucy and Liza, two very precocious little one-year-olds. They knew of our baby-making blunders, so they were eager to celebrate our adoption breakthrough with us. After some general niceties when we got to their place, I almost immediately asked where the bottle opener was. They stayed in the living room exchanging typical how-have-you-been-isms like normal adults do, while I rushed to the kitchen to free the wine from its glass prison.

In my haste, I neglected to cut the aluminum wrapper—I went straight for the cork. Although I knew only the truly desperate pull the cork through the seal, I decided I wasn't above it. *Embrace your inner wino.*

I poured us all a healthy glass of Cabernet Sauvignon. Speedily unscrewing the cork from the screw, I went on to deliver it back into the bottle to keep it fresh for the next glass. As I twisted the cork, my thumb passed by the traces of the ragged wrapper which I had neglected to cut off.

I looked at my thumb in disbelief. I was bleeding.

Hurrying over to the sink, I ran some water over it in order to assess the damage. It was definitely a cut, about an inch long.

"Uh…anyone have a band-aid?" I said.

In the other room, I could hear Kiersten ask Kara, "What did he just say?"

Weeks of walking on eggshells, being hyper-careful about everything I touched to ensure a quality print on every finger, and I cut it on a wine wrapper. Worse yet, I did it exactly six days before we were to travel to Immigration Services to be fingerprinted by the very electronic fingerprinting machines that our social worker had warned us about for their inability to get past nicks and cuts.

I started to laugh, seeing the obvious irony in not being able to drink for so long during the in-vitro process, and then putting my adoption process in jeopardy with a bottle of wine.

Kiersten? Not so much.

"What did you do?!" she exclaimed, seeing me holding my bloodied thumb in the sink.

"Well, I sort of cut myself."

Looking around the kitchen, she asked, "On *what*?!"

"See, this is kinda funny—I actually did it on the wine wrapper."

I could see the panic start to overtake Kiersten.

"It'll be fine, hon—trust me. I'm sure Janet was exaggerating about those machines," I said.

Kara jumped to the rescue, grabbing a band-aid and some Neosporin.

Kiersten wanted to see the extent of the cut before I covered it up. It was just off the pad of my thumb, but it definitely ran through some of my print. It wasn't a clean cut, either; it entered at an angle, filleting some of the skin off.

Trying to remain (and induce) calm, we moved into the living room to sit and drink our glasses of wine. I did my best to completely ignore the cut on my thumb, but I knew it wasn't good. I started to wonder what the going rate was for bribing a federal official during a routine fingerprinting.

Vince declared that dinner was ready, so I got up to open another bottle of wine.

I cut the wrapper off first.

CABANA FOR
IMMIGRATION SERVICES

Our plan was to arrive at the Center for Immigration Services in Yakima (central Washington State, for those of you West-Coast-challenged) as soon as they opened. We had heard of nightmare day-long experiences with excruciating wait times, so we wanted to ensure we were one of the first in line. Unfortunately, Yakima is about four hours away from where we lived, so it would mean leaving at about 3:45 in the morning. Despite our best intentions, we didn't get out the door until about a quarter to five and although I drove like they were giving away free cases of Makers Mark to the first 50 customers, we didn't get there until about 8:45.

I can't speak for Kiersten, but as I looked at the facility, it was not the building I had envisioned. Something with a name as intimidating and lengthy as "UNITED STATES CENTER FOR IMMIGRATION SERVICES" ought to be housed in a very institutional-like facility—either all brick or concrete and steel, a minimum of 12 stories tall in order to cast an oppressive shadow. But this place had the un-original architecture of an ill-conceived 1960s-era cabana-hut with shingled siding as well as a shingled roof. If it weren't for the windows, this sad, shaggy little building would have had the general appearance of a Hungarian sheepdog.

The security guard at the door was young and heavily tattooed. He would only allow us to enter one at a time as he patted us down and waved a metal detector in front of us and behind us. The hand-cannon on his belt made me a little uncomfortable. At the very least, it seemed excessive. Once inside, I understood the need for so much security. They were obviously fearful that someone was going to abscond with one of their folding chairs, or perhaps take off with a handful of pamphlets on how to get your Green Card. Yeah, that's sarcasm you're hearing.

The whole place couldn't have been more than 20 by 20 in size, with recently-waxed, gleaming white linoleum floors. There were about eight rows of metal folding chairs, all turned towards the 14-inch television which was mounted high on the wall, so as to discourage anyone from touching it. Someone must have tried, however, because there was a poster, which was actually larger then the television itself, hanging from it, reading, "PLEASE DO NOT TOUCH TV OR ATTEMPT TO CHANGE THE CHANNEL." I couldn't figure out how someone might attempt to change the channel *without* actually touching the television, but perhaps the USCIS folks didn't like to assume anything when it came to issues this important.

We took a number and sat down. There were roughly ten other people there, all craning their necks skyward to watch the moving figures on the modest picture-box. Not being a huge fan of daytime television, I continued to scan the room out of general curiosity. To my side were massive photographs of George W. Bush, Michael Chertoff, and Michael Brown. Apparently, Homeland Security oversaw Immigration Services. The Hurricane Katrina mess had recently happened, and I couldn't stop thinking of GW saying, "You're doing a heckuva job, Brownie!" in assessing the efforts in New Orleans. Suddenly, I was very glad the security guy was there to protect me.

My options were pretty thin, and I had forgotten my book, so I joined the other lemmings and started staring at the tube.

"Welcome back to the show," Martha said. "Today we're joined by Jennifer Garner, who is very clearly pregnant."

Boy, that time in the big house didn't take away your power of observation, Martha Stewart.

The two of them were standing adjacent to a kitchen island, well prepped for some kind of dessert-making escapade.

"We're also joined by some other pregnant women today," Martha said.

Oh, goody.

"In fact, every one of our studio audience members is currently expecting."

You have to be fucking kidding me.

"It's our pregnancy special!" Martha yelled.

The crowd roared as the camera panned over all of their bloated, pregnant, and wildly clapping bodies. Thrilling theme music was cued.

Once the audience members regained their composure, Martha made another announcement. "Well, that's not all.

I have some exciting news for all of our audience members. Each and every one of you will receive a complimentary Petunia Picklebottom diaper bag!"

Bedlam erupted. Thrilling theme music returned.

I looked at Kiersten. "Unbelievable," she said.

A loud gong filled the room and I realized a number had just been called. I looked at the digital reader board, which displayed "07". I looked at the number in my hand. 12. Since we'd been here, we'd moved up exactly *one* number. I decided to get up and re-read the sign beneath the television just to make sure it didn't say "PLEASE FEEL FREE TO TOUCH THE TV OR ATTEMPT TO CHANGE THE CHANNEL."

No dice.

We were stuck here watching Martha Stewart and 300 pregnant women make cookies for the next hour.

*   *   *

The gong rang and I finally saw "12" displayed on the reader. My heart jumped up into my throat—we were up. We approached the window with our paperwork and a check for $580. It turned out an I-171 ain't cheap, and there was really no economic mechanism to bring the price down—it wasn't like there were competitor Immigration Services we could go to. Sam Walton hadn't yet figured out how to offer I-171s at a huge discount.

We offered our three months' worth of paperwork over to a stern, petite woman wearing a navy uniform complete with a US flag and shiny badge. For some reason, I was terrified of this lady. She started thumbing through the stack, taking what she wanted and stamping, stamping, stamping them with authority. I looked around, trying to figure out where we put our hands through this glass, which seemed impenetrable, in order to do the fingerprinting. She grabbed her microphone and spoke to us through the glass. "Make your check out to the United States Center..." Kiersten handed her the check, already filled out to the USCIS. Who did this woman think she was dealing with, anyway?

She took our check through the small crack in the class and said, "Okay, everything is here—take a seat and they will call you for your fingerprinting."

Take a seat?

Terrific. More waiting.

Maybe the next program would be a Martha Stewart special featuring the delivery of every baby of every audience member. *"Remember, folks, some cultures actually eat placenta! Look for my new 'Martha Stewart Does Multicultural Recipes' book at Kmart this fall."*

We sat back down, and I noticed people being called into and out of a room flanking the main hall. This must be the fingerprinting room. I decided to time it—each fingerprinting took 18 to 20 minutes, so it wouldn't be long before we were called. My hands started to sweat as I inspected the cut on my thumb, wondering if we had just driven four hours and endured the single most irritating television show on the planet in order for them to tell me I had to come back to get re-fingerprinted after I soaked my hands in a tub of Vaseline for a month.

"Barr?!" the woman yelled.

"You go," Kiersten said. "Good luck."

I was led to a computer and told to sit in front of what appeared to be a miniature copier. My hands were cold and clammy. I speculated that this was how convicted criminals behaved as they were being connected to the polygraph.

"Okay, I'm going to just dry your hands real quickly and then we're going to take your fingerprints," the attendant said, as she applied a small green towel to my palm and fingertips. It had the texture of a chamois leather cloth used to dry cars at detail shops. She dropped my whole hand on the scanner. A light passed by on the machine and on the screen to my right, I saw the scan of my hand, prints and all. She grabbed the other hand—the one with the cut thumb—and went through the same routine. I turned my thumb enough that the scanner wouldn't pick it up. My other set of prints appeared on the screen.

This is cake! What the hell was Janet talking about?

"Now we just need to do the individual prints," the attendant said.

"The individual prints?" I asked.

"Yeah—did you think you were done?" she snorted. "We need to take a scan of every one of these little guys," she said as she waved my index finger in front of my own face.

Oh, boy. Okay, this is what Janet was talking about.

"Try to relax now. I'm going to roll your fingers over the surface until the computer gets an accurate reading," she said, taking the very thumb with the cut on it in her hand and placing it on the screen.

"How will we know when the computer gets an accurate reading?" I asked.

"It will make a little 'beep' noise and it will lock in on the print."

My future relies on a computer beeping. Terrific.

Starting with the good side, she began to roll my thumb over the scanner. I could see the print appearing on the screen to my right. As she got to the other side of my thumb, I tensed up, resisting her just enough to keep my cut from being discovered. She pulled a little bit more and I froze up, refusing to let her continue, hoping the computer had seen enough, praying this hunk of high-tech machinery took pity on me.

The print didn't take. "Hmm…okay, you really need to relax," she said. "Go ahead and shake your hand out a bit…just shake it out." She demonstrated how to "shake it out" and we sat together, flailing our hands in the air.

After I had done the hokey-pokey with her just enough, apparently, she grabbed my thumb once again and started the roll. We were getting to the bad side of the thumb, and again, I was fighting her. I couldn't tell if she knew I was doing this, but I simply wouldn't let her go any further. I fixated on the screen, attempting to conjure up The Force, which I had been convinced I had ever since seeing *Star Wars* as a five-year-old, *willing* the computer to accept this print.

Bleep! The computer burped.

"Well, there you go—congratulations, the computer took that one," she said. "Maybe the rest will go easier now."

"It did?" I asked, my hands damp and cool.

"Yep, it took," she said. "Boy, are you nervous? Your hands are freezing."

"Must be poor circulation," I said. "I think I'm ready to relax and do the rest, though."

One at a time, she rolled each finger over the screen. The computer would bleep in agreement as every digit passed.

"That's it—you're done," she said.

"I pass?"

"You pass."

I got to the door, and the ear-to-ear grin on my face told Kiersten immediately that I had gotten away with the crappy thumbprint. I could see her sigh in relief as she grabbed her purse and started back for her turn with the beeping computer.

"So, no problems with the thumb?" she whispered.

"Well, I'll tell you about it later—but everything worked out."

"Thank God," she said.

"Good luck in there," I said. "Let me know if she makes you do the hokey-pokey."

As I sat back down, I looked up at the television, where Jennifer Garner was admiring her new Petunia Picklebottom bag. It was almost an involuntary reaction by now, so I couldn't really help it.

"What the hell are you looking at, Petunia Picklebottom?"

BEAUTIFUL FLOWER

"Do you remember the names that I liked for girls?" Kiersten asked.

"I just recall a long list of turn-of-the-century old names that you bounced off of me," I replied as I merged with traffic back onto the freeway.

She reached over and turned the volume down on the Strokes CD to which I was obviously paying more attention than to her.

"Well, yeah—but remember how I was thinking we would use Celia because it seemed more Scandinavian?"

"I vaguely recall that, yes," I said, notching the volume up just a tick so I could make out some of the incessant whining of Julian Casablancas, who sounds as if he is near passing-out-drunk 24-7. But it works with the music, don't get me wrong.

"Well, how do you feel about the name Flora?" she said.

The trip to Immigration Services had evidently had a liberating effect on her. Submitting a petition to bring an orphan—*our daughter*—to the United States lifted a burden, a sense that all of this might not come to fruition. Her guard protected her from another disappointment, and this visit served to tear it down.

She finally started to *picture* her. Our kid. We'd have a daughter. Suddenly, her maternal instincts kicked in and the first order of business was to name her, or at least develop a new list of options for a child who would not be blond and fair skinned, but one with dark hair and darker skin than ours—and these characteristics apparently impacted Kiersten's range of possible names.

"I thought Flora was out," I said.

"No, remember I tried to get Vince and Kara to use Flora because I've always pictured it on a dark-haired baby?" she said.

"Oh yeah! Our kid probably won't have anything but dark hair until she turns sixteen, rebels against everything we say, and dyes her hair green."

"She will *not*!" she replied, aghast at the image. I laughed at the look on her face.

"I think Flora is a great name," I said. "But don't we want some kind of culturally-relevant name in there somewhere?

"I was thinking about that too," she said.

Surprise.

"I always liked the name Flora Mae... so we could change the M-a-e to M-e-i, which is Chinese for 'beautiful.' Her name would mean *beautiful flower*."

"Flora Mei," I said, giving it a test-drive. "Flora Mei. Flora Mei. I think it's great. I'm in."

And just like that, we named our daughter. Even though we didn't know her, what province she would come from, where or why her parents chose to abandon her, or how old she'd be when we finally picked her up and looked her in the eyes for the first time—she had a name. It felt very real. Flora Mei felt very real, like she was waiting for us as we waited for her. And it felt so good to see Kiersten smile.

*   *   *

By the time we got home, it was already near 5:00. After eight hours of driving and two hours of stress and watching Martha Stewart and 300 pregnant women, I'd be damned if we were cooking dinner. I made a few suggestions for a celebratory meal on the town, and we decided to go to a local brewery. Really, it was the only option I gave Kiersten as I invoked my new mastery of The Force on her after my miracle with the electronic fingerprinting machine.

These aren't the droids you're looking for.

You want to go to the brewery.

She wanted to change her clothes, so I took the opportunity to get online and check baseball box scores to see how my fantasy baseball team was doing. I also wanted to test out The Force on my shortstop, Jimmy Rollins, to see if I could will a few stolen bases out of him—but I got the sense that The Force only works in person.

I saw Kiersten head downstairs, to touch up her makeup, I assumed. I decided I could use a change of clothes as well, and walked into our bedroom, hoping the clothes I had in mind weren't in a giant heap on the floor of my closet, as they often were.

Standing in front of our mirror, sizing up my new outfit, I noticed a change in the landscape of our room.

Something was missing. To my right, there was a bare spot, outlined by an accumulation of dust that was truly shameful. I turned to see the missing item had simply been moved. And cleaned. On our bed sat the Petunia Pickle-bottom bag that for the last year had been relegated to our bedroom corner, collecting dust as well as disdain from Kiersten for what it represented. This bag, this overpriced sack of wool that I had badmouthed repeatedly, had been thoroughly cleaned, its pockets inspected, embroidery appearing meticulous as ever for the discriminating mother.

The bag was set free. With it, we were set free.

I stood there, stupid grin on my face, marveling at what had been accomplished since this morning. We had filed the petition to bring our daughter here, I finally passed the fingerprinting, I learned to hate Martha Stewart and Jennifer Garner, we named our little girl, and Kiersten turned a corner on her way to motherhood and healing.

And then the bag name hit me: 'Fond of Flora.'

For crying out loud.

The bag knew all along.

THE MICHELIN MAN

Kiersten was in Chicago for a conference, but the news was too good to wait. I called her cell phone from the mailbox.

"Hello?" she said.

"Guess what just arrived?" I asked.

"The I-171?!"

"Yep—we're good to go," I said. "Or rather, *she* is good to go."

"That's wonderful!" she said. "That's it, you know—we're totally done. All we have to do is send that along with some other paperwork to be authenticated and we can send off the whole dossier."

The receipt of the I-171 while Kiersten was gone meant I had a job, however. The I-171 was the only document that was not sent in the dossier as an original—you had to have a copy notarized. Considering my experience with notaries, I viewed this task with a fair degree of trepidation, but I decided to give it a shot nonetheless.

I arrived at my bank, made an appointment, and subsequently waited for the notary to come out from the sea of cubicles in the back of the building. I had this lingering sense that this wasn't going to go well, so I brought a copy of the instructions that were sent to us from the adoption agency, just so I had something official to corroborate my request.

"I can't notarize a copy," the notary said.

I'm shocked.

"Well, this is for an adoption—I have the paperwork here that says…"

"No, you don't understand—a notarization is certifying an original document," she interjected.

"If you'd just give this a look, maybe you'll see that it's pretty standard to notarize a copy of a document such as this one." Adding a little extra emphasis, I continued, "The original is supposed to stay with us – it's *what we take to China to show their government that we have the authority to bring one of their orphans to the United States.*"

"I understand that," she said sternly as she read over the agency instructions. "But I just don't think… I don't think…" stammering as it became increasingly clear that she could notarize a copy. "…I don't think…"

I couldn't agree with you more.

"Well, fine—I guess I can make a copy *for you*, and then if I *notarize that*, I'll have a reasonable assurance that it's a true copy of the original," she said.

I was simply stunned by her logic. I honestly began to wonder if I was being secretly filmed. Could anyone who held a steady job at a bank possibly be this thick? I couldn't even begin to think of how to either make fun of her or corroborate her line of thinking, so I just nodded. She took my original I-171 to make a copy, and I almost got up to follow her for fear that she'd shred the original and then rationalize it by saying, "Well, I'll notarize the copy for you!" But I thought it would be too rude to shadow her Xeroxing.

To both our surprise, she returned with the original. What's more, she managed to make a copy of the side with the print on it, though I'm sure she'd burned through a half dozen sheets of paper, confused as to why they kept coming out blank until the intern explained how the machine worked.

"This copier is broken!"

"Try turning the original face down."

After a brief moment of panic because her ink pad was dry (yes, she had left it open after the last notarization), she borrowed one from the cubicle next door and I had a notarized copy of our I-171. I thanked her for working with me under the strange circumstances, and finally decided to tell her about the smear of barbeque sauce she had on her chin.

"You've got a little something right here," I said, motioning to my own chin.

"Oh, God—how embarrassing. How long were you planning on waiting before you told me?"

"Well, until just now, so about 15 minutes."

She was mortified, but it wasn't a big deal. After all, I was just impressed she didn't drool.

*   *   *

As soon as she returned from her conference, Kiersten took the I-171 copy, as well as roughly 20 additional documents that had already been notarized and certified, and Federal Expressed the lot, along with a hefty check, to the Chinese Embassy in San Francisco to be authenticated. Days later, it was all returned with the fancy red wax seal on the familiar rice paper.

Kiersten delicately organized every last piece of documentation. She double-checked each item against a checklist provided by our agency just to make sure everything was there. For good measure, she triple-checked the exact order in which everything was supposed to be.

Any delay in processing the dossier could mean months of additional waiting for the "log-in date" to be registered. The log-in date was, essentially, the point at which you got in line. Everyone processed after you was behind you, unless, of course, your name was Madonna or Angelina Jolie. The agency communicated with you in log-in-date terms as they articulated how long it might take to get matched with your child: "We've recently received the next batch of our matches—all those with a LID of 4/29/05 to 6/29/05 have been matched," and so on. It allowed you to gauge your wait. And my wife hated to wait. So this document was going to be perfect.

The last dossier decision to make was what pictures, of the many photographs we had set aside, we would ultimately enclose with the paperwork. It felt a bit conceited to have such grave concern for what picture graced your dossier, but we learned from our social worker that the way you presented yourself could have a major impact on the child with whom you were matched.

According to Janet, matches were not made based on the kinds of qualifications that you might imagine. We were a younger adopting couple, which meant we qualified for the youngest kid available—typically six to 12 months. But beyond that, the match process had more to do with how you looked. The officials sat down with your dossier, examined your pictures, and literally looked around the orphanage for the best possible match with the couple.

I had a hard time believing this, and challenged Janet to explain how it really works. She decided to use an anecdote to articulate her point. As the story went, there was a couple who went to a colleague of hers for adoption in China. One of them was apparently overweight. Overweight as in needing gastric-bypass surgery. Big people would call this person big. Anyway, the pictures they had around the house and those that were taken for the dossier were well before the weight loss that occurred as a result of the surgery. By the time they were about to adopt, this individual was well within a "normal" weight range and the surgery was considered to be a huge success.

When they received the picture of their "match"— their soon-to-be daughter— they were equally shocked and delighted to see a ten-month-old whose rolls started just beneath the chin and didn't end until her feet. As Janet described it, "They matched them with the Chinese equivalent of the Michelin Man." After all, who else could better relate to this little chunk than an adult chunk?

These kinds of matches were apparently the status quo. Tall and skinny, big head, little head, big ears, short and small features, light skin, dark skin, happy face, grumpy face, you name it—they would try to match a Chinese child that most resembled your features. All this seemed particularly ridiculous to me because, after all, we're Caucasians adopting a Chinese baby—there was no degree of similarity that was going to change that, was there? Regardless, the point was that you wanted to present yourself well in your photos, so the process should be taken seriously. Fortunately for us, nobody took the process more seriously than my wife. So she picked out a number of gems, bundled up our dossier, and sent it off to the agency. Everything from this point was in their court—our work was finished. The big wait was on.

Ah! What would the world be to us
If the children were no more?
We should dread the desert behind us
worse than the dark before.

– Henry Wadsworth Longfellow (1807-1882)

OFFSPRUNG

The week in which we sent off our dossier was a festive one. My mother-in-law went on a baby-crap-buying frenzy. There were little shoes, darling onesies, adorable tiny hats ... pretty much anything you could find at your neighborhood Carter's store, she bought. Kiersten spent time at a local home-improvement store, picking out shades of pink for the baby room. We received calls from my parents, my sister, and many other loved ones, asking for details. We very much felt that we had 'a baby on the way.' I credit our families for rallying around the adoption and making us both feel so good about bringing this little girl into our family. She didn't know it, but this kid was going to be spoiled, big time.

Two days after we sent the dossier, we were notified by our agency that it was received. They would now use a team of individuals to thoroughly inspect it to ensure there was nothing therein that would put our adoption in jeopardy after sending it to China. This process would take them approximately seven to ten days to complete and we'd hear later if any changes needed to be made, but considering the efforts of our social worker and Kiersten's meticulous approach, I didn't expect to hear any major misgivings from the agency.

The work week gave way to the weekend, and Kiersten and I spent much of our Saturday afternoon poking around antique stores, searching for just the right hunk-of-junk old dresser that could be restored into a baby changing table. It was our goal to create one for under 40 bucks, as we'd seen changing tables in those Pottery Barn Kids magazines for as much as $600. Can you imagine spending that much cash on a platform to wipe a butt? That much money for a changing station better include a robotic ass-wiping mechanism. We generated lots of ideas, but unfortunately came up empty handed.

Kiersten was feeling under the weather, as she had for the last few days, so she retired to the couch for a nap. I was on a recent health kick, so I took the opportunity to abuse our elliptical machine for a half hour of low-impact, joint-happy cardio. Feeling particularly spry, I threw in a two-mile jog on the end of my workout. I couldn't let my knees think they'd get off that easily.

I stopped by the couch to check on Kiersten. It turned out my extra effort had led to an unanticipated problem. "You stink," she said.

"Well, you've got bad hair," I retorted.

"Very funny."

"I'll go shower and then we'll get a bite to eat, okay?"

"Okay. I'm going to just nap for a little while longer," she said.

I was standing in the shower when I heard Kiersten open the door to the bathroom. I couldn't see exactly what she was doing as I was blocked by the shower curtain.

"What are you doing?!" she said to me with a distinct urgency in her voice.

Confused, I looked down at myself in the shower. *What am I doing? What do you mean, what am I doing?* Turned out, I was standing there, taking a shower— nothing out of the ordinary there.

"Uh, I'm taking a shower," I said, continuing to lather my face with soap. "What did you think I was doing?" I wondered if she thought I was in here refining the art that I'd honed on the suicidal couch back at the clinic.

"WHAT ARE YOU DOING?!" she said again.

Now I was just plain confused.

"What's going on Kiersten? What's wrong? Is there something wrong with Bella?"

There was no reply, but instead she shoved her hand inside the shower curtain. My eyes were blurred with water and soap, but it looked like she'd pushed the thermometer in for me to look at. I deduced that she had some kind of high fever, which wasn't abnormal for Kiersten. Considering how erratically she was behaving, I figured I needed to take this seriously, so I turned to wash the soap from my eyes.

"Just a second," I said.

Vision cleared, I rotated back to the thermometer and took it from her hand, expecting something in the 101 range.

Why is she so prone to high fevers?

But this wasn't a thermometer at all. It was a small, plastic device with a digital display, much like our thermometer. But this one didn't register temperature. I threw the curtain open to find Kiersten, eyes wide, tears cascading down her face, both hands covering her mouth. She looked both terrified and amazed. She was trembling as if she were hypothermic, shaking uncontrollably.

I pulled my towel off of the bar on the wall and wiped my eyes dry, blinking repeatedly to ensure I was seeing what I thought I had just seen. But there was no mistaking what this little contraption was telling me.

Kiersten was pregnant.

I looked at her, suspicious of the validity of this revelation.

"So it's wrong then," I said.

In between hyperventilating breaths, she said, "There... are no... false... positives!"

"Well, then, who is the father?"

"Michael!"

So there I was, naked, water cascading off me on to the tile floor, a pregnancy test in my right hand, left hand on top of my head, mouth agape, immobilized with disbelief.

All I knew was that if this thing was accurate, someone was going to pay dearly for the months of quitting booze and beans. And I couldn't stop wondering if this meant I needed to buy another flipping Petunia Picklebottom bag.

EPILOGUE
(SEPTEMBER 2010)

I'm nursing a hangover thanks to the bottle of Bookers bourbon my buddy Bryan purchased for my 38th birthday. In this small room, I know I reek of alcohol, but I don't wear cologne and there's really a limit to the number of places you'll smear gel deodorant in an effort to mask the booze. And I'd be damned if I missed this appointment.

"Do you want to know the gender?" asks Rachel, the ultrasound technician.

"We already know," says Kiersten. "We paid for an early ultrasound at 17 weeks."

This is our 20-week ultrasound appointment and, coming as a shock to absolutely nobody, Kiersten couldn't wait 20 weeks to know the gender. There was a private business that provided creepy 3-D baby pictures via high tech ultrasounds, but it turned out that they could also do a normal ultrasound and provide a gender check. So we paid 75 bucks to give Kiersten an extra three weeks to buy crap and start planning every day of the kid's life from birth to high school graduation. The result was fairly obvious to the technician.

"It's a boy," Kiersten says.

"Well, congratulations!" says Rachel. "I can double check, though, I have been known to overrule early ultra-sounds. It's rare, but it happens."

Rachel has never been wrong about the gender of a baby in her career, and you could sense the pride she took in that fact.

Sitting in this familiar room, I can't help but smile ironically and think about our path getting to this place. Three months ago, we were told by our adoption agency that our wait for our baby girl will likely be another two to three years. After waiting for the better part of four years now, it didn't come as a tremendous surprise that China's matches for adoption had recently slowed to a downright trickle. Some of our documents had already expired once and we had to get fingerprinted yet again in order to re-up the I-171 petition to bring an orphan to the United States. Every year seemed to demand a renewal of one costly form or another in order to keep our proverbial foot in the adoption door. We still desperately wanted to see our adoption through, but it was hard to stay optimistic.

Kiersten had exchanged e-mails with our social worker Janet to size up the situation, on the outside chance that Janet had any insider information that our agency couldn't tell us. Janet checked her files to see when our log-in date was because she understood that there was an expiration date on our original application, the one that took Kiersten months to put together, including the home study and all associated paperwork. According to Janet, our adoption application would expire in approximately 18 months and at that time, we would literally start from scratch, although we wouldn't lose our place in line with China. This presented a significant predicament. A moral, philosophical, monetary, and very personal dilemma. What would we do after 18 months? Could we possibly just walk away? Could we possibly bear another application process? Could we endure another three years of waiting?

So much had changed during this wait already. Gus was starting preschool in the fall. Cancer had taken my mother away. I had taken a new job (yes, so I wouldn't go friggin' crazy) and Ike was just taking his first steps at 15 months. And now we were planning for our third boy, all kids conceived without the process we were told we would absolutely need in order to have a biological baby. What a bizarre path indeed.

Sitting here in this room, head pounding, stinking of booze, I sense the guilt that I've felt since we had little Gus Anders. Throughout the struggle to have a baby via IVF, I felt a sort of kinship with other couples fighting a losing fertility battle. I'm reminded of it every time I see a childless couple. It may very well be their choice to not have kids, but I always wind up giving them that pathetic telegraphed smile that says, "I'm one of you." All of us survived in our collective hatred for the boink-and-baby insta-families.

I'm still that guy screaming at unattainable green bottles of liquor from the driver's seat. Still the guy whose heart sank every time his phone rang. Still that guy praying to whatever God would listen to help Kiersten through this. But I felt like I'd switched teams, been given a gift that I couldn't understand. In reality, I had changed teams, but I still wanted anyone struggling with infertility to know I was with them. I am, I thought. But I know I'm not really welcome. Not anymore. Now we're "fucking normal breeders."

Inexplicably, here we are looking at the translucent outline of bones and guts of baby Barr #3 on a flat-panel Samsung TV. Gus was our ridiculous little miracle, we thought. But then came Ike, with hardly much sheet-time whatsoever. And this one—made in literally one week, practically by accident. How could this be, given the odds we faced five years ago? It was all so strange that Ken actually wanted to re-test my swimmers to see what the hell was going on under the microscope. An invitation to visit my friend the suicidal couch, not to mention Geena Davis, was difficult to turn down.

Rachel squeezes the goo over Kiersten's bare belly, now getting quite round, and pushes the wand down to start the ultrasound.

"That's fine, go ahead and make sure it's a boy—we wouldn't want any surprise…"

"Well, case in point," Rachel interjects, "you see these three little lines right here?"

Using a track ball mouse, she points to a blob that could have been a sea anemone for all I knew. But Rachel did know.

"This is a little girl," she says.

I start laughing out loud. Kiersten shrieks.

This life refuses to be predictable.

It's really quite perfect, don't you think?

Your children are not your children.
They are the sons and daughters
of Life's longing for itself.
They come through you but not from you,
And though they are with you,
yet they belong not to you.

- The Prophet, Khalil Gibran

ACKNOWLEDGMENTS

I wouldn't have ever finished this if not for the encouragement, feedback, and creativity of a great number of individuals. In no particular order, I'd like to thank the following: Emmett Branigan, Antionette Estes, Amy Blackwood, Cory Blackwood, Kara Kisena, Paul Peterman, Elizabeth Aarstol, Kenneth Walker, Sam and Jessica Chang, JoAnn Vesper, Raynu Peterman, Jeanne Gaffney, Julie Craddock, Luci Grubbs, Bryan Grubbs (even though you didn't read the damn manuscript), Doug Heatherly, Yael Abel, Laurel Leigh, Julie Simon, Sarah Lunde (especially because I spaced our meeting), Ted Askew, Pamela Mahoney Tsigdinos, Andy Anderson and Karen Anderson (for being my biggest fan).

A very special thanks to Kiersten for continuing to stick with me.

And apologies to Geena Davis.

ABOUT THE AUTHOR

Michael Barr is more frequently found writing about baseball at Fangraphs.com, RotoHardball.com, and complaining about being a Seattle Mariner fan at Marinerlog.com.

You can find him on Twitter at @michaelcbarr, blogging about whatever occurs to him as relevant or interesting at www.swimmingcircles.wordpress.com, and of course, you can find him on Facebook.

4824233R00202

Made in the USA
San Bernardino, CA
09 October 2013